THE VALUE OF LOYALTY

by
Margot Webb

THE ENCYCLOPEDIA OF
ETHICAL BEHAVIOR

THE ROSEN PUBLISHING GROUP, INC.
NEW YORK

Published in 1991 by The Rosen Publishing Group, Inc.
29 East 21st Street, New York, NY 10010

First Edition

Manufactured in the United States of America

Library of Congress Cataloging-in-Publication Data

Webb, Margot.
The value of loyalty / by Margot Webb. —1st ed.
p. cm.—(The Encyclopedia of ethical behavior)
Includes bibliographical references and index.
Summary: Using real life situations for examples, explains the concept of loyalty as a necessary force, connecting people in a confusing world.
ISBN 0-8239-1243-4 :
1. Loyalty—Juvenile literature. [1. Loyalty.] I. Title.
II. Series.
BJ1533.L8W43 1990
179′.9—dc20

90-43817
CIP
AC

Cover Photo: Courtesy of The Image Bank
All Other Photos: Wide World Photos

About the Author

Margot Webb has been a teacher and a counselor to children in California, in the Los Angeles area.

Born in Germany during the Holocaust, Mrs. Webb managed to escape with her parents in 1939, but the rest of her family died in Auschwitz.

Settling in California, Margot studied opera and was fortunate enough to appear in a few productions. She entered the University of Southern California with the express purpose of continuing her musical career but was waylaid by marriage. She and her husband, a Hindu from India, lived for three years in Bombay before returning to the United States.

Widowed, she first began to teach. She then took a master's degree in counseling and began work on a doctorate at the University of Southern California. Remarried now, Mrs. Webb lives with her husband, an editor, in the Los Padres Mountain region, fairly close to Los Angeles.

Contents

Introduction

Darlene huddled in a corner of the bathroom. In the other rooms of the house sudden laughter exploded, rock music blared, conversation hummed — Richard's party was a success!

But here in this sterile white bathroom Darlene felt nothing but terror. She was sick. Everything was spinning around her. She put her head on the cool tile floor and closed her eyes. Never in all her fifteen years had she experienced such misery.

Darlene heard the insistent knocking on the door, but it sounded far away.

"Darlene, open up!" Bernice cried. "What's going on?"

There was no answer.

Richard's party continued in full swing. No one noticed Darlene's trouble.

Bernice felt she had to do something. She had to help her best friend. It was obvious to her that Darlene was sick or in some kind of trouble.

"Richard," she called over the noise of the rock music, "Richard — we must help Darlene!"

Richard was dancing with Sue, eyes closed, body moving rhythmically.

"Wait till this record's over," he shouted at Bernice.

"But there's no way to get to Darlene. She's locked herself in the bathroom."

Richard left Sue and went with Darlene to the closed door.

"Maybe I should get my parents," he suggested after rattling the knob. "They're upstairs, and they don't want any problems."

Bernice nodded, but she was upset. She had thought she could always get through to Darlene, until now. Darlene hadn't really wanted to come to this party. She was too shy, didn't feel she could match up — but Bernice had insisted.

And now Darlene, locked in the bathroom, had become unavailable to her. Richard's parents would become involved, and Darlene might be even more miserable.

Just then Richard's father came with a screwdriver and managed to unlock the door. The music had stopped; the party quieted down. When the door was opened, Darlene was seen lying on the floor, passed out. Her open purse showed a bottle of liquor, half empty.

"I thought I told you there was to be no drinking at your party!" Richard's father shouted.

"And there wasn't," Richard answered.

"Until now." The father's outrage frightened Bernice.

"Sir, we only had sodas — and Darlene never did this before. In fact, she is very shy and didn't want to come."

"Let's take care of the child first," Richard's mother said as she came down the stairs.

Richard picked up the unconscious Darlene and put her on the couch.

The guests began to leave, mumbling their thanks to Richard. The party was ruined. Only Bernice stayed.

"I'm seventeen and have a car. I'll be glad to take Darlene home. We've been enough trouble already."

"Let me call her parents before you do anything," Richard's father said. "They have to know what their daughter did." He walked purposefully to the phone.

Bernice shivered. She needed to hear Darlene's story. She was her best friend.

"No answer — no one home," Richard's father announced in

a disgusted tone. "Let's put some ice on her head, get her to come to. Then you can take her home."

"Do you think that's wise?" Richard's mother asked. Just then, Darlene's eyes opened and a moan escaped her lips.

"I'm sorry," she mumbled, looking from one face to the other. "Where's everybody?"

"They've all gone home," Richard answered. "How do you feel?"

"Awful — and sorry. How can I apologize?"

"By throwing that liquor away," Richard's father replied.

Bernice was busy getting their coats. She gently helped Darlene to sit up and put on her coat.

"Please have her parents call us when they get home," Richard's father insisted. "And stay with Darlene until someone arrives at her house."

"I will. I'm sorry about your party," she turned to Richard, then put her arm around Darlene and slowly helped her outside.

Once the door of the house closed, Darlene retched in the street. Bernice gave her tissues to clean her pale face and helped her into the car. She drove a few blocks and parked on a quiet street.

"Darlene, where did you get the liquor?" Bernice questioned.

Darlene sobbed, her head in her hands. "I've been afraid to tell you, Bernice, but every time I get scared in school or my parents are mad at me — or I have to go to a party like Richard's — I take a little drink to calm my nerves."

"That was no little drink," Bernice shuddered. "The bottle was half empty."

"I was just more scared than ever."

"You need help, Darlene. We must tell your parents."

"No!" Darlene's shriek was one of absolute terror. "You're my best friend. You must be loyal to me."

Bernice was stunned. "But I am being loyal, Darlene. You need help. I'll explain to your parents how scared you are and that you drink for false courage. I'll be with you all the way."

"That's not loyalty!" Darlene's mood had changed to an ugly anger. "You're supposed to accept me the way I am."

"I do. But I can't accept your behavior. It's making you sick. I have to do the right thing. I *am* your friend, and I hope some day you'll understand my loyalty to you. I'll always be your friend, and one who will get you help when you need it."

Bernice started the car and drove directly to Darlene's home. The lights were on in the house, and Bernice, holding Darlene firmly, rang the bell.

PART ONE

The Meaning of Loyalty

— FAITHFULNESS AND TRUTH

Many people use the word "loyalty" without giving much thought to what it really means. This section will explore different views of loyalty.

Is true loyalty just going along with others? For your loyalty to have meaning, you must know who you are — what you are being loyal to — and why.

CHAPTER 1

Is Loyalty a Static Value?

People talk about loyalty all the time, and as they talk, the differences in what they see as loyalty are enormous.

In school, every morning before classes begin, students are expected to recite the Pledge of Allegiance to the United States. In many high schools the disembodied voice of the principal comes over the loudspeaker and directs everyone to put his hand over his heart . . . "I pledge allegiance . . . . " Students say with practiced boredom. The principal is satisfied that he has promoted loyalty to the country in a matter of twenty seconds. Hardly anyone has any idea what the pledge is about, nor do they care to give it any thought.

- Do you know why you are expected to recite the Pledge?
- Do you feel it is necessary to say it daily? Or does the frequent recitation rob it of its intended ideals?
- What are you promising to do when you give your Pledge?
- What would most people say if you questioned all or part of it?

You would probably get a response such as, "Well, of course, you must say the Pledge. It is an act of patriotism."

For these soldiers on Memorial Day, the American flag is a symbol of the country to which they have pledged their loyalty.

Is just saying something an act? Is patriotism to be trusted merely by falling in line with school policy? Are you becoming more patriotic with the frequency of the recital?

Let's look at what you are really saying. "I pledge allegiance." You are promising loyalty. And to what are you promising that loyalty? Surely not just to a flag. You are taking a solemn oath to the symbol that the flag represents. You will be faithful to your country, which, in turn, promises you liberty and justice.

Implicit in the Pledge is an oath to you — that this country will return loyalty for your loyalty.

What is expected of you in your promise of allegiance? You are to be faithful, not just in wartime as a soldier, but more importantly, in upholding the peace and laws that protect us all. Liberty and justice follow naturally.

It sounds as if loyalty always has built-in expectations of behavior. If you do a wonderful thing, then your friend, your parent, or your country will have to return the favor. Not so. Loyalty is not a static value. In many instances you cannot demand anything of it. You can give loyalty freely with no expectation for yourself. It is an act of faith, of believing in an idea so strongly that you will do a great deal to make it work.

In the introduction Bernice knew that helping her friend was an act of loyalty despite Darlene's drunken objections. Was it possible that Darlene would be angry with Bernice in the days that followed Richard's party? Yes, of course! However, Bernice's act as she walked her friend to the front door to explain matters to Darlene's parents was an act of faith and loyalty. She expected nothing in return.

Loyalty as a Complex Value

You can see that loyalty is not a simple value. It is complex. The many ways in which loyalty shows itself are examined in this book. Your interest in reading about a value that has been argued over for thousands of years by thinkers and philosophers, by priests and rabbis, by families and close friends, shows that you are ready to become a person to whom loyalty is an important ingredient of life.

- Do you believe there are different kinds of loyalty? Is loyalty a value with more than one dimension?

Jason and Carol Take a Lifetime Step

Jason, a twenty-three-year-old architect from Michigan, had recently graduated from college with a master's degree. He looked forward to building beautiful homes that would be safe and functional. Already a company in Arizona had offered him a good job, and it seemed that his dream was beginning.

Just before graduating, he had met Carol, who was starting her career as a nurse.

At first they dated each other only occasionally. Both Jason and Carol had many friends and were busy people.

The more they saw each other, the better they liked and understood each other. Finally they realized they were in love. They talked about their future lives: Jason as an architect, Carol as a nurse in the field of surgery.

On the day Jason received the letter from Arizona he proposed marriage to Carol.

He took her to dinner at a fine restaurant, and just before dessert he reached into his pocket for a small box containing a sparkling diamond ring. Carol flushed with joy, and as she put on the ring she whispered, "I'll love you forever."

After dinner they went to Carol's house. She still lived with her parents because she had been saving money to furnish her own apartment.

She made coffee and brought it to Jason in the living room, where he sat on the couch, deep in thought.

"Changed your mind already?" she teased.

"Of course not," Jason protested, "but I was so happy about our engagement that I completely forgot to tell you something."

"What is it?" Carol became apprehensive.

"Oh, nothing terrible. Rather something wonderful. I've been offered a job in Arizona with an architectural firm I've admired for a long time. I'd like to take it, but it would mean leaving Michigan and our families and friends."

Carol became very quiet and thoughtful.

"You're disappointed, aren't you?" Jason asked. "I should have told you about the job first."

Carol looked at Jason earnestly. "Tell me something, darling. If I had been offered a position as head surgical nurse in a New York hospital and you hadn't gotten this offer, would you have been willing to move to New York with me and look for a job there?"

"Of course, I would. Are you questioning my loyalty to you?"

In a marriage ceremony the bride and groom promise each other support, understanding, and loyalty through good times and bad.

Carol laughed. "Not at all. But you were questioning mine with your worry about our moving to Arizona."

Jason was amazed. She was right! They wanted each other's happiness and fulfillment.

"There are many hospitals in Arizona," Carol said, admiring her ring's gleam. "And as far as our families are concerned, we can visit them and they can visit us."

"You are wonderful." Jason took her left hand into both of his own. "We will be a family — a new family when we take our marriage vows."

"In sickness and in health, until death do us part," Carol answered, using the old words from the wedding ceremony.

In the varied expressions of loyalty, this story illustrates still another way to show faith in person and therefore in a relationship.

In marriage, it is essential that two people freely give their loyalty to each other. One does not have to sacrifice to prove loyalty. On its deepest level, the value of loyalty lies in understanding, in giving and supporting, and above all, in truth.

- How do you think Jason felt when he sat alone in the living room, waiting for Carol to make coffee?
- What did Jason learn from Carol about loyalty?
- Do you believe that open communication is an act of loyalty to the person you love?
- How else is loyalty shown in a marriage?

Loyalty is complex, as you can see, but what is at the bottom of all the faces of loyalty?

CHAPTER 2

Truth to Oneself

Before you can be faithful or loyal, it is important to know what you are being faithful to. Even more difficult is knowing yourself and being completely truthful about who you are.

You might begin to look at yourself and answer the following questions:

1. Am I usually fair?
2. Do I think of several alternatives before I make a decision?
3. Do I trust my friends?
4. Do my friends trust me because I am loyal to them?
5. If I don't get my way, do I take my anger out on someone else?
6. Am I a contributing member of my family?
7. Do I like myself?
8. Am I a valuable person?
9. What are my fears?
10. What are my strengths?

You can see that these questions are only a part of your thoughts about yourself and your conscience.

Loyal people are people of great value. They are the ones who help to make our lives meaningful and who inspire us.

Johnny's Experience at Bat

Johnny had always been a baseball fan. He collected baseball cards, watched games on TV, and attended games at his junior high school.

He seemed to have friends who liked baseball, too. But some of them snickered behind his back because he was overweight.

"Hey, Johnny, why don't you join the Babe Ruth League?" they teased. "If a ball hit you, you wouldn't even feel it."

Or, "Johnny, why don't you become bat boy and run off some of your fat?"

Johnny began to realize that some of his friends were not loyal to him at all.

He would go home, go to his room, and think about his problem. He felt sorry for himself and often cried secretly.

One day Allan, whom Johnny had known since elementary school and frequently ate lunch with, asked Johnny if he could come over. Allan had never made jokes about Johnny's weight.

The boys walked to Johnny's house together. Allan was curiously silent. Engrossed in their thoughts, neither boy spoke.

When they reached Johnny's house, no one was at home. Johnny's mother worked until four o'clock and his father did not come home until six.

As soon as they were inside Johnny said, "Let's raid the refrigerator," as he carelessly tossed his jacket and school books on the living room couch.

"I'm not hungry," Allan said, "but thanks just the same."

"I have a great video of the Dodgers in training camp," Johnny suggested, mouth full of cookie, head in the refrigerator looking for more food.

"I've come to talk to you, Johnny," Allan said, "because I'm your friend. There'll be a spot on my Babe Ruth team in the spring, and I thought you'd like to join."

The refrigerator door closed abruptly.

"Who — me?" Johnny's laugh was bitter. "The fat boy everybody makes fun of? No way!"

"Let's go up to your room and talk, please," Allan insisted.

"O.K. O.K. I just wanted a snack."

As the boys started upstairs, Allan remarked, "You left your jacket and books on the couch."

"So what? One more thing for Mom to get steamed up about," Johnny answered.

"Well, don't give her the chance. She's probably tired when she gets home," Allan suggested. "Go on and get your stuff."

"You sound like our P. E. Coach giving orders," Johnny grumbled, but he did go down and retrieve his things.

"So, what do you have to say?" Johnny started once they were seated cross-legged on the bed in Johnny's room.

"I'd really like you to be on my baseball team," Allan began. "You have a great personality when you're in a good mood, you know a lot about the game, and you have until spring to take care of your problem."

"What problem?" Johnny started to say, but immediately went into a slump. "I just don't know what to do about it."

"Do you know why you eat?" Allan asked kindly.

"Never thought about it."

"Well, start thinking. Get to the truth of it."

Johnny sighed. "When the other kids make fun of me, I just come home and eat. Things seem better for a little while."

Allan was quiet, but his eyes encouraged Johnny to go on.

"I guess I'm kinda lonely, too. Nobody's home when I come back from school, so I watch TV and eat. It seems to keep me company."

"Does your mom have to work?" Allan asked gently.

"Yup. She's paying big bills for my sick grandmother who needs a nurse."

"So your mom really has no choice."

"I guess not," Johnny mumbled.

"I've been your friend since fourth grade, Johnny, and I'd like to help."

Johnny looked into his friend's face and realized that Allan was speaking the truth.

"O.K.," he said, "I just don't know how to start."

Allan laughed. "Consider me your coach at home, not giving

orders — just suggestions. But first, a promise. Will you join the team in the spring?"

"I might," Johnny answered, tossing a handful of cookies into the wastebasket.

The boys sat for two hours making diet charts, exercise charts, and schedules for homework.

"I'll come over three times a week and run with you and toss the ball. Then we'll check your diet chart. I know it won't be easy," Allan said.

"Thanks a lot for being so good to me," Johnny called as Allan left.

"What are friends and teammates for?" the answer came quickly.

Johnny looked in the mirror and for the first time saw himself truthfully. "I'm a person who feels sorry for himself and has never made room for anyone else. I'm going to change, starting with helping my overworked parents."

He ran downstairs, washed the breakfast dishes, emptied the garbage, and picked up odds and ends.

When his mother came home, he gave her a big hug. "Mom, sit down," he said excitedly. "I've made you some coffee! I'm on a diet! Allan will help me! I might even join the baseball team! I'm going to help you more around the house!"

His mother laughed, "Hold it a minute. You're going to do what?"

Johhny repeated his promises more slowly.

That night in bed, he thought about Allan's loyalty. He, Johnny, would match Allan's faith in him by trying to change and become a better friend and son.

By spring, a fit, slim Johnny joined the Babe Ruth League and made his first home run after only a month of training.

Allan slapped him good-naturedly on the back.

Johnny's parents were in the stands and applauded both boys. They had taken the afternoon off for the first game of the season.

Instead of laughing and jeering at a weight problem, a good friend can help you turn your life around and become the person you want to be.

The loyalty of one friend had brought about a change in Johnny. The change was based on Johnny's facing the truth about himself and on the faith Allan had in him.

- How did Allan show courage in his loyal behavior to Johnny?
- What did Johnny learn about himself?
- How are truth and loyalty interrelated?

Don't be afraid to look at the truth. It is the highest part of you, the part that will see you through difficult as well as happy moments in the years to come.

If you can face the truth about yourself or a situation in which you find yourself, your path is made clear. You will realize your own value, and you will automatically know where your loyalties lie.

Throughout history people have searched for the truth that would lead them to goodness, to honor, and to loyalty. Now you too are searching for your own truth to give meaning to your life.

Conscience Can Lead the Way to Loyalty

Because loyalty has such an enormous impact on others, you probably realize that it does not come easily.

It is a value that requires a great deal of thought and reflection. Before you decide to whom to be loyal and how to show your loyalty, your conscience will undoubtedly play a great part.

Morgan's Test

From the beginning, Morgan had trouble in physics class. She was an excellent student in her other subjects, but physics made no sense to her at all.

She talked to her teacher, who underlined important concepts in her textbook, but when she left school and tried to study in her room, all the explanations left her. Nothing had any meaning.

Morgan even approached her parents and asked for a tutor.

"You must be joking," her father said. "You're practically an A student in every subject."

"But, Daddy . . ." Morgan wailed.

"Just relax. You're too tense about physics," her mother chimed in.

"I propose a toast," Morgan's father smiled, lifting his wine glass. "To Morgan's A in physics at the end of the semester."

Morgan was shocked and dismayed. No one wanted to help. It seemed to her that everyone expected her to do well in all subjects. "Well," she thought angrily, "it isn't that way at all."

As the semester went on, Morgan was helplessly lost. She asked another student for help, but all she got was an indulgent little smile.

"You don't need help, you're the school brain," she was told.

Meanwhile, her parents praised her studiousness to the point where Morgan felt she would be disloyal to them if she failed to produce a perfect record of grades.

One day she ran into Mike in the grocery store. He had graduated from high school the previous year.

"How's it going?" he asked.

Morgan hung her head.

"Hey, Smarty, is it a boyfriend? What's wrong?"

Morgan answered, "No, nothing like that. I'm up for the eleventh grade scholarship cup, but I know I'm not going to make it. I feel like I'm letting everybody down."

Mike leaned against the shelves, scrutinizing her. "But you always . . ."

"Got As," Morgan finished for him. "But not this time," she continued. "Physics has me beat. The more I study, the less I understand."

"Hey, Morgan, don't worry. I can help you. You're in Mr. Long's class, aren't you?"

"Yup," she said, "and he tried to explain the stuff to me, but it didn't register."

"I just told you I can help," Mike repeated.

"You have time to tutor me?" Morgan asked hopefully.

"You don't need a tutor. I have something even better. Come to my house tomorrow after school, and your worries will be over. You'll get your scholarship cup!"

The next day Morgan rang Mike's doorbell. His mother answered the door.

"Mike told me he could help me with my course in physics," Morgan said a little hesitantly.

"But he graduated last year," his mother seemed surprised. "It wasn't his favorite course. How can he help?"

Mike came running downstairs. "Mom, I still have all my physics notes and papers stashed in my closet. Come on up to my room, Morgan."

"Leave the door open," his mother admonished.

."Gee whiz, she thinks every girl is a potential girlfriend," Mike said good-naturedly, leading Morgan upstairs.

After rummaging around in his closet, Mike held up his physics notebook triumphantly.

"Here it is," he announced. "Mr. Long gives the same tests year after year. And he puts the correct answers over our wrong ones. You can have all my tests with all the correct answers. Just study those, and watch physics go by like a breeze."

Morgan could hardly breathe. She was shocked and pleased at the same time. What was the right thing to do?

"But that's cheating, Mike," she finally gasped.

"Why?" Mike's easy response relaxed her a little. "You'll have to study!"

"But I won't understand it. It'll just be memorizing."

"And what's wrong with that? You're still putting in an effort." With that, Mike stuffed the notes and tests in her backpack.

"Come on," he laughed, "let's get a hamburger and a milkshake. I'm starved!"

"Thanks, Mike," Morgan tried to smile. "I appreciate what you're doing. I've got to get home now, or Mom will wonder where I am. May I take a raincheck on the hamburger?"

"Sure," Mike answered and waved to her as she left.

During dinner, Morgan thought of the test papers in her backpack. Her stomach began to hurt.

"May I be excused?" she asked her parents.

"Run along," her mother said, "I'll see if you're better in a little while."

Morgan went to her room and took out all the physics tests. "I'll get the scholarship cup. My folks will be proud of me," she thought.

She began to look at the test questions. They made no sense to her.

Suddenly she heard her mother's footsteps and hid the papers hastily. When her mother opened the door, Morgan's face was flushed and hot.

"I think you may have a fever," her mother said.

"Sit down, Mom, please. I'm not physically sick. I have a problem with my conscience."

Morgan told her mother about the whole miserable struggle with physics, including the "cheating papers" as she now thought of them.

"I just can't use them, Mom," she ended, crying. "I can't do anything so wrong. I thought if I got the scholarship cup, I could show you and Dad that I tried my best and that I'm loyal not only to my studies, but to both of you."

Morgan's mother stroked her hair. "I've never been as proud of you as I am now. You have learned something far more important than a high school physics course. You have learned that before you can be loyal to others, you have to be true to yourself. And you're a girl who can't cheat."

As Morgan looked up, she saw her father standing in the doorway.

"Your mother is right," he said in a hoarse voice.

"I feel so wonderful, thanks to both of you," Morgan cried.

"No," her father said, "thanks to you."

They ended the evening making confetti out of Mike's physics tests.

Morgan crept happily into her bed that night.

- Why did Morgan feel it was wrong to take the papers from Mike?
- A little part of Morgan wanted Mike's papers. How did she think she could overcome this feeling about cheating?
- What did Mike tell her to make her comfortable about using his papers?

- When did Morgan's struggle with her conscience come to a climax?

Conscience and the Small Inner Voice

If a decision feels right and good to you with no nagging doubts, chances are excellent that you will not hurt yourself or others. Loyalty and conscience are links in the same chain of truth.

Every day, in big and small decisions, your conscience speaks to you. Listen to it, because the small inner voice is your voice of loyalty.

Think of your favorite song. Each note builds on the others until there is a beautiful piece of music. Loyalty is like a happy, flowing song made up of the harmony of truth, of conscience and its inner voice, and of faith.

If the inner voice is ignored, the harmony is disrupted. The satisfaction that could be yours is spoiled. It will cause pain even at an apparent moment of triumph.

An Athlete Ignores His Inner Voice

During the 1988 Summer Olympics, an athlete who had worked for years, for many hours each day, ignored the Olympic motto and his loyalty to the Games. The motto: "*Citius* (faster), *Altius* (higher), *Fortius* (stronger)" meant that athletes were to achieve world-record excellence by participating in the greatest physical competition.

The young runner in the 1988 Games was a favorite. Many thought he would win a Gold Medal and become the world's fastest runner.

During training his coaches persuaded him to take steroids, which would make him even stronger, even faster.

The Olympic Committee, which assures that the fair rules of competition are kept, forbids the use of steroids. The young runner knew that, but his desire to win outweighed his loyalty to the sport, to the other athletes, and to the country he was representing.

Having been stripped of his gold medal at the Seoul Olympics, a tearful Ben Johnson admits at an inquiry that he cheated and lied about his drug use.

Can you put yourself in the position of the Olympic runner? Imagine standing on the victory stand as a Gold Medal winner. A ribbon is placed around your neck, flowers are pressed into your hands, your national anthem is played, your flag waves behind you, and people are cheering and crying. They are proud to be a part of your victory.

But a small inner voice, the voice of conscience, is nagging at you, ruining your moment of glory because it was not your strength or commitment or loyalty that allowed you to win. It was your greatest weakness — a weakness that allowed you to ignore the truth, to take steroids, and to have false strength. Your moment of moments is spoiled.

Juan Antonio Samaranch, President of the Olympic Committee, said, "The Olympic Games offer an opportunity for the youth of the world to gather in a spirit of friendship, enjoying each other's company as they learn the importance of values . . ."

If you had been the great runner, puffed up by steroids, would you have understood the meaning of loyalty? Would you have been true to yourself?

Strangely enough, you probably could have won without the illegal steroids, had you listened to your inner voice and not to the persuasive voice of the coach.

- Why is it more important to be loyal to the ideals of competition than to win?

You can see how loyalty is made up of more than one simple word. Loyalty is a value that must be shared with others. When you are loyal, you feel good about yourself. You know who you are. You have every reason to like yourself and to be proud of yourself.

CHAPTER 3

Fanaticism

Fanaticism means unreasonable enthusiasm. The person who is a fanatic is moved by a frenzy of zeal without looking into the cause of it. His behavior is extravagant. He boasts about his unreasonable beliefs and, unfortunately, all too often acts on them.

Who Are Fanatics?

Fanatics are people who are desperate to belong to a group and who need to feel superior to others.

For instance, the terrorists of the Middle East, who blow up buildings and kill themselves in the process, are fanatics. They have been programmed to believe that what they do gives their people more rights and a better way of life.

But you know that nothing good comes of such violence. The terrorist is unreasonable. He is full of hatred against one group or another. He is a fanatic.

Many people in the last few years have joined cults and

started supposedly "religious" organizations. Some of these cults made animal sacrifices and moved on to human sacrifices. Members of cults were killed. Still others stayed on, believing, without thinking, that their leaders were right. They thought that the murders (called "sacrifices") were part of their rites. These people are fanatics.

Skinheads, people who shave their heads and carry weapons against minority groups, are fanatics. They don't stop to realize what they do and why. They feel they are better than others and therefore have the right to hurt and punish those who are different from them.

During the Spanish Inquisition, hundreds of years ago, thousands of people were put to death because the fanatics thought they could see evil in their eyes or in their behavior. The fanatics tortured their victims, burned them at the stake, and imprisoned them in dark dungeons in the name of being right. Everyone else was wrong. It never occurred to them to question those in command.

Throughout history fanatics have made others' lives miserable by being unreasonable and simply following along with a powerful group.

Can Fanaticism Pose as Loyalty?

The big problem is that sometimes whole nations and their governments become fanatic.

If the citizens of such countries fail to obey unreasonable rules, they stand to be put to death by firing squad, placed in a concentration camp, or "eliminated" (killed).

The fanatics, however, see themselves as true followers of their hurtful cause. They will do anything, as long as they belong. And thus they are motivated to continue their bizarre behavior.

When people stick to a cause that does evil instead of good, loyalty is completely misplaced.

These Nazi soldiers were unquestioningly loyal to Hitler and did not consider the gross inhumanity of his ideals.

Hilter and Nazism

In 1933 Adolf Hitler became the dictator of Germany. From the beginning, his fanatical speeches were frightening to many and thrilling to others. He shouted slogans at the top of his voice during speeches, and the people responded by shouting back, "Sieg Heil, Sieg Heil." It was a sort of victory cry.

Germany had been very poor, and Hitler promised "his" people a better, richer life — if they followed his orders.

He began with the children and young men of Germany. They wore uniforms of the Hitler Youth. They were taken on camping trips, given food when food was scarce, and, most important, they were taught two things:

1. Not to question Hitler's orders.
2. To hate people of all minority groups.

Many of the young people had Jewish and other minority group friends but now were no longer allowed to be with them. If they disobeyed Hitler's orders, their parents were arrested and punished. The parents had to prove their "loyalty" to Hitler by bringing up their children to follow his orders.

You can see that Hitler was a fanatic, and some Germans struggled with their consciences whether to follow him or remain loyal to their friends.

In the end, most Germans went to the side of fanaticism. They became Nazis, soldiers of Hitler, and followed orders blindly.

Hitler wanted to conquer the world and keep the human race white, blond, and blue-eyed. He called his people Aryans, and those who were not Aryans were tortured and killed.

Still the Nazis followed along. There were parades with hundreds of huge, blood-red flags bearing Hitler's and Germany's insignia — the swastika in black in the middle of the flag. The soldiers sang loudly in praise of their leader as they marched with powerful steps in heavy black boots.

People watching these parades often shivered with fear, but they decided to adopt a false loyalty and join the hectic fanaticism.

"If you are loyal," Hitler proclaimed, "you will tell us who does not like our government, and we will take care of them."

His form of "taking care" was putting people, especially Jews (men, women, and children), into concentration camps. There they slowly starved to death while they worked with their weak bodies. They had to carry rocks, dig mass graves, bury the dead. If they were musicians, they had to play their instruments while others died.

Hitler's doctors performed terrible surgeries without anesthetics, and the screams of the "disloyal" or the Jews could be heard for miles around.

Hitler's "final solution" for getting rid of people he did not want in Germany was to build gas chambers. His soldiers would herd forty or fifty people at a time into the chambers, turn on the gas, and through a closed window laugh as the victims slowly choked to death.

Hitler decided that his Nazis were loyal.

- Can you see how fanaticism and true loyalty fight each other?
- When Hitler used the word "loyal," he meant something else. What word can you substitute for the fanatic's meaning of loyalty?

The Ku Klux Klan

The Ku Klux Klan began to form secretly after the Civil War to prevent equality for blacks in the South. But those who joined were so full of hate that they decided to be anti-Catholic and anti-Jewish, as well.

By 1915 the secret society was completely formed in Georgia, and its members became really active during the 1920s. They murdered and terrorized people who were "not our kind" — not only in the South, but all over the United States.

What did the Klan members really believe in, with their misplaced loyalty to each other? They believed in white supremacy. They thought that they, being white, were better than anyone else. The Ku Klux Klan claimed that the white race was superior to any other race.

Why was their loyalty misplaced? For one thing, the mem-

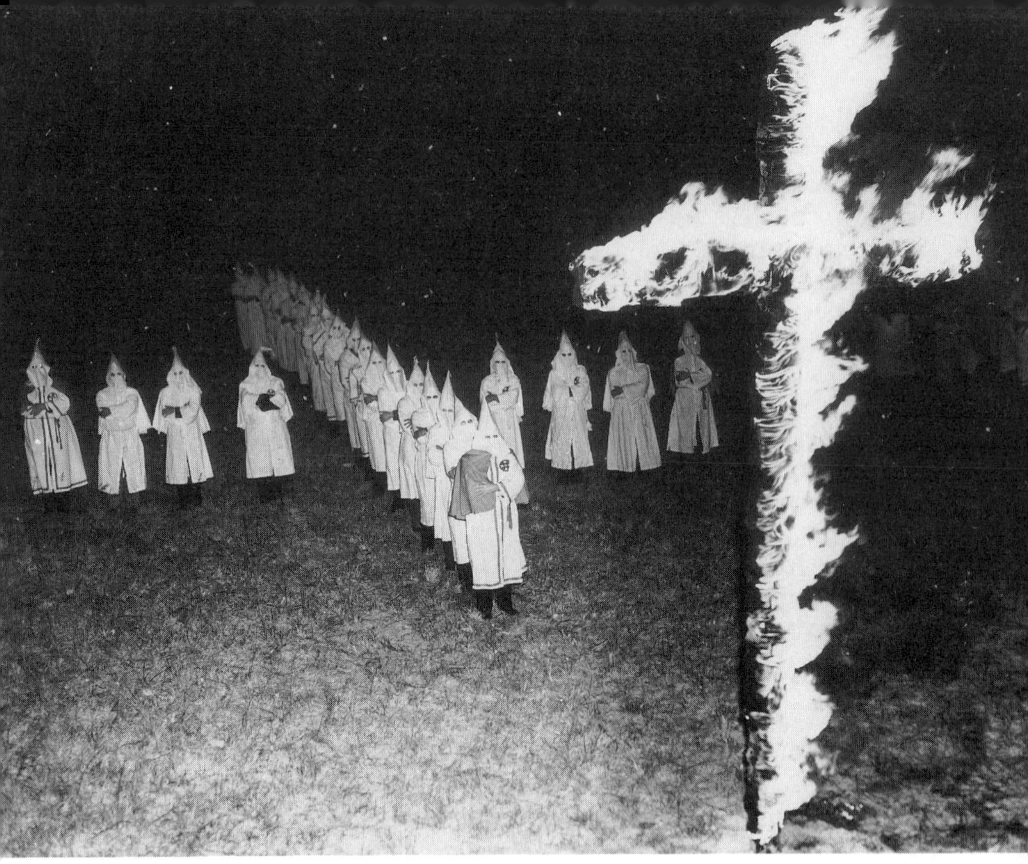

White-robed Ku Klux Klansmen burn a 15-foot cross during a private ceremony.

bers of the Klan ignored the fact that, first and foremost, they belonged to the human race. Being white or of a certain religion did not make Klan members better. Not being those things did not make others worse.

The Klan members acted as though they had chosen to be born into their race, forgetting and being disloyal to anyone who wasn't like them.

What did they do? The Klan members dressed in white robes and pointed white hats and covered their faces so that no one could recognize them. Most of their activities were carried on at night, so that they could frighten their victims and not be caught so easily.

The Klan picked out the houses of black families (or Catholics or Jews) and burned huge crosses on their lawns. Often they set fire to the houses of their "enemies."

At other times they lynched the man of the house. In a lynching, a mob seizes a person, accuses him of a crime, and without a trial hangs the person accused. The Klan might also tie a black man to the back of a horse, and as the horse ran the screaming man would be dragged through the streets until he was dead or near death.

Since Ku Klux Klan members were sworn to secrecy, they had the mistaken idea that they were loyal to their race and to each other.

We have seen earlier that loyalty must include trust and faithfulness.

- Is it being loyal to be faithful to a group that considers itself better than the rest of the world?
- Why is the loyalty of Klansmen to one another of no value?
- What similarities do you find between Hitler's Nazis and members of the Klan?

Unbelievable as it may seem, the Klan still exists in the 1990s. It is not as powerful as it used to be, and many members are known to police and the FBI, but every so often the newspapers report the burning of a house of a Black, of a Jew, or of a Catholic. The telltale burning cross is frequently left behind.

CHAPTER 4

Gray Areas

As you can see, being loyal is not always easy. It involves your feelings, your careful thought, and your ability to be trusted, as well as to trust. Loyalty involves decision-making. Sometimes it is hard to tell what needs to be done.

For instance, should you maintain loyalty or allegiance to old friends?

Your answer is probably a resounding, "Yes." Why should you even consider dropping old friends you may not have seen in several years?

In most cases your loyalty is necessary if you really considered the person a friend. Being unable to see someone for years is no reason to become disloyal.

However, what happens if your friend has changed over the years, changed his values, attitudes, and ideals? If he is now the opposite of you in matters you consider good and just, should you still be loyal to him?

This is what is called a gray area. It is fuzzy, not as clear as you would like it to be. You may ask, "Who deserves my loyalty?"

Jane: The Story of a Long Friendship

Betty and Jane had first become good friends in high school. Both girls liked music, both were somewhat shy around boys, and both liked to read.

They were together almost daily after school and on weekends. But there was a problem. Jane came from a very wealthy family, and her father did not approve of Betty. He was afraid Jane would insist that Betty come to the many "exclusive" parties they were invited to in San Francisco and she would not be smartly dressed. Betty's family had come from Europe, and although they were highly educated, they struggled for a living and could not afford expensive clothes.

Jane took every opportunity to tell Betty how much her father disliked their friendship. Finally Betty suggested that they end it because Jane's stories about her father hurt too much. To Betty's surprise, Jane said, "But I don't like my father. I tell you these stories so you can understand me better. Please don't break up our friendship."

Betty was persuaded, but whenever she was at Jane's house for dinner she noticed how her friend flattered her father. It was harder and harder for Betty to believe that Jane did not care for him.

When Betty realized that Jane was disloyal to her, as well as to her father, she finally broke off the friendship.

Ten years later Jane and Betty met accidentally in a restaurant. Jane's enthusiasm at the chance meeting became infectious. They sat together and caught up on the stories of their lives, their husbands, jobs, and children. They laughed as much as they used to, and Betty enjoyed herself tremendously.

At that moment, one of Jane's friends approached the table.

"Hello, Jane. Ready to go shopping?" the friend asked.

"Sure," Jane answered, standing up. "By the way, this is Betty. I used to know her in high school."

Jane's friend smiled coolly at Betty. "How do you do? Excuse us, but we must hurry."

Jane waved a quick goodbye and left Betty with the bill.

Two years later, Betty received a sad letter. Jane had a handicapped baby and worried constantly what might happen to the baby if she become sick or died. In the letter, Jane recalled the good times with Betty and invited her to dinner the following Saturday night.

"We can talk about old times," Jane wrote. "It'll be so wonderful to see you again. You've always been my best friend, Betty. I just wasn't grown-up enough to realize it," the letter concluded.

- Did Jane deserve Betty's loyalty?
- What did Jane really want?
- Why do you suppose Jane called Betty, rather than one of her new friends?
- Is it possible that Jane was sincere in her letter?
- How would you have handled the situation if you had been Betty?

Have you had a good friend, as a child, who had to move away? At first you probably wrote letters to each other, but perhaps later you both tired of it.

Whenever you thought about your friend in the other city, however, you remembered him or her with warm feelings.

Peter and David

Peter and David lived across the street from each other in Los Angeles. They had played together since kindergarten. Their parents even went on summer vacation trips together.

Although they were of different races, they told everyone they were cousins. In fact, they felt as close as brothers. One day twelve-year-old David ran to Peter's house, tears streaming down his face.

"What's wrong?" Peter asked, anxiously.

"We're moving to Virginia," David now openly sobbed. "My dad is going to work in Washington, DC."

Peter was shocked, but after an hour of talk they decided to ask David's parents if David could live with Peter and finish school in California.

David's mother listened to their pleas. She then asked them to sit down and gave all the reasons why David couldn't stay: He needed to be with his family. His mom and dad loved him, too. But, she brightened, "You can come to Virginia to visit as often as you like."

"And David can come to Los Angeles." Peter's mother had heard the commotion when David first came over. The two mothers convinced the boys that it wouldn't be the end of the world. They would simply have two homes — one on each end of the country.

The boys did visit each other and remained friends for many years. When they reached young adulthood, Peter became successful in public communications, whereas David at twenty-three still didn't know what he wanted to do. He lived at home and didn't work.

Finally Peter felt that his loyalty to David should include helping him. He flew to Virginia and asked David to pack his bags and come live with him in California.

At first David, too comfortable at home, didn't want to do it, but after days of talking about the future, David went with Peter. The pep talks about study and work continued, and at last David enrolled in a local university. He moved out of Peter's apartment to be near the campus, and four years later he graduated with honors.

Today Peter is a successful communications director — and David is a well-known TV sportscaster. They are still good friends. Loyalty and trust worked hand in hand.

- Did David deserve Peter's loyalty? Explain your answer to your innermost self.
- Although Peter was successful before David was, did Peter ever let his feelings of loyalty down?
- What was the difference between Jane (see previous story) and Peter?

You can understand loyalty as a tremendous value — a value that can make a difference in the lives of our friends and our families. Loyalty is not always easy, but if it is given freely and honestly, it is a gift.

PART TWO

Why Is Loyalty Necessary?

Can you imagine a world without loyalty? A world in which everyone did as he pleased without regard to others' needs and feelings?

It would be a world without love, a world of confusion — a selfish and lonely place.

CHAPTER 5

Trust

We need to feel safe. Only when we feel safe can we accomplish what needs to be done.

A newborn baby must be pretty frightened on its first day of life. All the lights, the noise, people talking, huge faces and hands coming near, are probably scary things. The difference between continuing fear or confidence lies in the way the baby is handled. Usually, the mother and father gently hold the baby in warm blankets, cradling him and cooing to him.

Soon the baby will trust the parents and from then on trust others.

Trust is an essential part of loyalty.

We need to trust people if we are to feel good about ourselves. In turn, we must be trusted.

Being Dependable

One way to go about this business of trust is to be dependable.

You have read stories in this book that show loyalty on a small scale — friend to friend, parents to child. These are the building blocks of a greater loyalty: loyalty to groups of people,

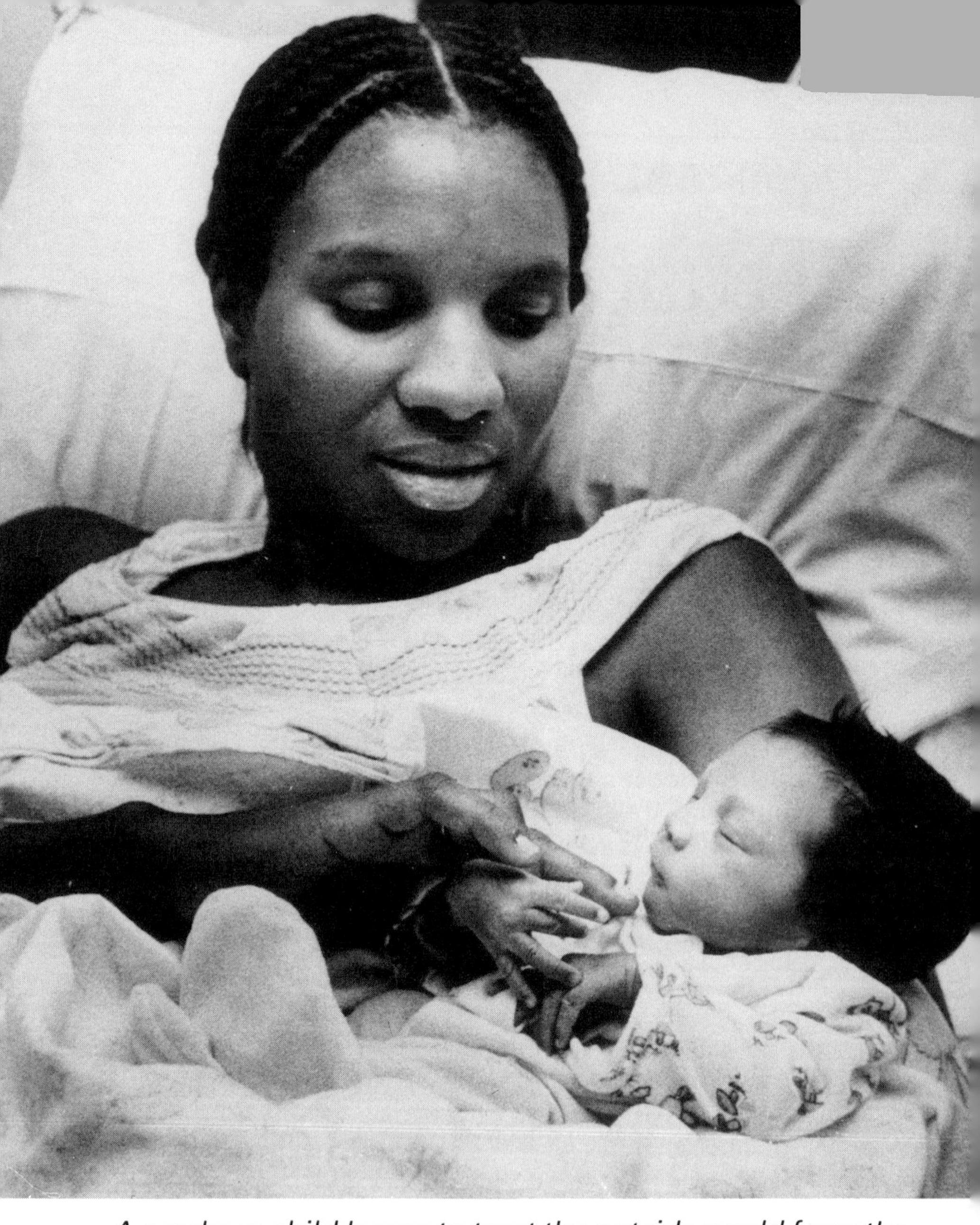

A newborn child learns to trust the outside world from the safety of her mother's arms.

to our nation, and ultimately to the safety of our world. We are about to climb loyalty's ladder.

When you are dependable as a young person, chances are excellent that as you continue to grow the scope of your values will increase and deepen. You will make a contribution just by being you.

Human beings cannot survive without a chain of love, trust, and loyalty. They would have to look over their shoulders in fear if this chain did not exist. They would not meet each other's eyes. They would live in a perpetual cycle of war with one another. Prejudgment (prejudice) becomes a key factor in the lives of people who live without love, trust, and loyalty — a path of fright, might, and hatred would become the way of the world.

Fortunately, you do not have such a terrible world to live in. You value important ideas, and what is more important than being real and true with one another?

CHAPTER 6

Loyalty in Families

The first place you learn loyalty as a very young child is in your family.

Have you noticed how your parents stick together when they are worried about money, about paying bills, about giving you the best education? They talk their problems over and try to arrive at a solution that will benefit you, their child. Often mothers go to work to help out with bills so the family will not want for warm clothes, comfortable housing, and nourishing food. At other times the father may take two jobs to make sure his family is safe and secure.

This kind of loyalty between parents and toward you, their son or daughter, will make you feel cherished. You know you can trust them, and it is a good feeling.

Many families, of course, do not have money problems, but they may have a child who is blind, deaf, or otherwise disabled. They look for the best care possible. They love their child and stick up for him or her in times of distress. They are loyal to their family.

Still other families may have no visible problems. People are drawn to them because they have a loving attitude toward each other and seldom speak an unkind word about members of the family.

A handicapped child can inspire a fierce love and protectiveness in other members of the family.

Of course, it is ridiculous to imagine that brothers and sisters of such families never fight with each other or argue. However, when disagreements come up, fairness in the argument is part of loyalty to one another.

Have you ever been at a park or playground and heard a brother and sister in a real screaming match? What happened when someone tried to interfere? More often than not, the brother or sister turned on the third person with, "This is my sister. Don't get mixed up in my family." What does that kind of response tell you?

Loyalty to Your Entire Family

Loyalty in families goes far beyond mother, father, and siblings.

Think of all the people in your family: grandparents, uncles, aunts, cousins, and more. Many families are so large that they have periodic reunions to see and touch each other again.

India has a system called extended family. Young and old live together in one house, and when someone needs care it is always available. People can stay in the midst of their family for life if they wish.

- How do you think old people feel regarding their safety in an extended family?
- Do you think the children feel safe?

How about children who grow up in a family where the parents are divorced? They may feel that their mother and father have not been loyal. But such parents may have had to deal with problems they didn't anticipate when they married. To preserve some sort of harmony, divorce was the only answer.

In John Gunther's book *Death Be Not Proud,* he tells of the long illness and death of his seventeen-year-old son. Gunther and his wife, Frances, were divorced, but when their son was diagnosed with a brain tumor they pulled together and were completely loyal to him. They spent a great deal of time with him, both separately and together. Gunther praises his former wife for giving her son the gift of fantasy and his "creative curiosity" and for being with him all the time.

Your first loyalty is to yourself. When you know you are a worthwhile person and respect yourself, then and only then can you reach out to others. If you are mistreated in any way by your parents or other members of the family, tell a trusted adult. In that way you actually help the adult who abused you to get help from a psychologist, minister, or rabbi. People who abuse others have a problem. If you bring the problem out in the open, it may be solved. In that way you show loyalty, not only to yourself, but to the abusive family member as well.

Fortunately, most parents do their best for their children. As the children grow up and parents become old, the children in turn try to help their parents. The circle of loyalty is complete.

- Can you think of at least five ways members of your family have shown you loyalty?
- How have you responded to your family?
- How many aspects of loyalty can you name?

CHAPTER 7

Loyalty in School

As a young person, you spend a great part of your life in school. School is almost like a second family.

It is there that you learn to read, to write, to do math, to play games, to make friends.

School is important because it is where a great part of your future is shaped. You find out wonderful things about the world. You meet interesting people. Your teachers and counselors show care, concern, and patience.

Patience with others is yet another part of loyalty. Most people who decide to work with students are very patient and helpful.

You in turn can show your loyalty to your school by doing your best and appreciating your teachers' efforts to make learning the wonderful experience it is.

Sometimes, of course, a student has problems; and if no help is available at home, he often turns to a teacher.

Two students express staunch loyalty to their teachers by supporting the strike action.

$TRIKE
SUPPORT
OUR
TEACHE
THEY
EED
RIKE!!

Jose Learns the Meaning of Loyalty

Eight-year-old Jose was in third grade. He was known as the class clown, disturbing everyone during lessons. He laughed out loud, grabbed pencils from others, and if he didn't get attention, he fell noisily out of his chair.

His teacher, Mrs. Sanchez, tried to calm him down, but nothing seemed to work. Then, at the class Christmas party, she noticed that Jose didn't eat anything but put all his goodies in a napkin.

"Why don't you eat, Jose?" Mrs. Sanchez asked.

"Oh, I'm not hungry. I'm going to take all this food home," he said.

After the bell rang, Jose offered to help clean up. Mrs. Sanchez was surprised, since it was the first positive move on Jose's part. She agreed to let him help her.

Whenever he thought the teacher wasn't looking, Jose found bits and pieces of cookies and cake and filled three more napkins to take home.

But Mrs. Sanchez had seen. When all was cleaned up she asked Jose to sit down.

"I wonder why you are taking all these cookies home?" she gently asked.

"Maybe my sister will be nice to me," he said. "My mother died and I live with my older sister. She hates me. She only loves her own kids."

"But she took you in," Mrs. Sanchez said.

"Yeah, because nobody else wanted me. When we eat dinner, I have to wait till everybody finishes. Then I get the leftovers. I want to bring her a present so she won't scream at me tonight."

Mrs. Sanchez sat thoughtfuly, wondering about the best way to help Jose.

Suddenly Jose reached in his pocket. "You look sad, Mrs. Sanchez. I have some crack. You can have it for nothin'."

Mrs. Sanchez kept calm, although she felt a shudder run through her. "Where did you get it?" she questioned.

"I have to sell it on the block, or the big kids from high school said they'd kill my sister. Then I'd have no house to sleep in."

"You don't have to sell cocaine. I'll help you, Jose. But first you have to trust me, believe in me. Do you?" Mrs. Sanchez became fiercely protective of Jose at that moment.

"I trust you," the child said slowly.

"Then I want proof. Throw your cocaine in the toilet. I promise I'll see to it nothing bad will happen." Mrs. Sanchez heard her words and hoped she was right.

Hand in hand, they walked to the faculty bathroom. Mrs. Sanchez watched as Jose took the packet of white powder from his pocket. He stood in front of the toilet where he was to dump the drug.

Mrs. Sanchez watched as Jose's face mirrored the emotions that struggled inside. His expression changed from fear to doubt and finally to determination.

"They might kill me, but I'm doing the right thing," he said.

He looked pathetically at Mrs. Sanchez, who nodded silently.

Jose stood for another few minutes. Then with a great effort he threw the crack into the toilet and flushed it himself.

"I'll stand by you, Jose." Mrs. Sanchez opened her arms, and Jose flew into them.

Here was an eight-year-old who had never been hugged — and now he was being hugged by his teacher, whom he had given much trouble.

Today Jose lives in a loving foster home. He now calls Mrs. Sanchez "Aunt Rosa." He is doing well in a new school, and, above all, he is safe.

He learned to trust one person and his life changed. His loyalty to "Aunt Rosa" has spilled over into loyalty to learning, to his class, and his school.

- How was Jose's teacher responsible for him?
- Can you remember teachers you have had who did more than just teach?

Fraternities and Sororities

Although their names imply that fraternities are brotherhoods and sororities are sisterhoods, they are actually exclusive clubs on our college and university campuses.

These fraternity brothers, pictured outside their house at a California university, were banned from campus activities because of their unacceptable behavior in a racial clash.

Many fraternities and sororities own beautiful houses near college campuses where students who were invited to join can live. They call each other brother and sister and are expected to be loyal to their fraternity or sorority.

Often, the way to get in is to be recommended by a friend or by a parent who belonged when he or she was in college.

Unfortunately, many of these exclusive clubs admit only students whose parents make a certain amount of money, or who come from "good" families, or even more sadly, who belong to a certain race.

The fraternity or sorority invites students to a party to be looked over. If the members like what they see, the hopeful students must go through a period of initiation during which they must do whatever they are told, and some of their "duties" are humiliating.

Once in the fraternity or sorority, however, they live in

pleasant surroundings, have parties, and are part of a group that considers itself just a bit superior to the rest of the school.

David and Arch

David belonged to the best fraternity at his university. Lots of boys wanted to join, but there were many restrictions. Only the wealthiest could afford membership.

David wanted to become a doctor, but in his sophomore year he had already had a great deal of trouble with chemistry.

Arch was in David's class, and chemistry was a breeze for him. He actually liked it!

One day David asked Arch to eat lunch with him at the student union. When they had sat down with their trays, David explained his problem with chemistry.

"I'm glad you told me," Arch instantly responded. "Let me help you. I can explain some of the formulas to you."

David was thrilled. "Thanks, I really appreciate that. Could we meet at the library tonight?"

"We can't really talk in the library," Arch answered. "Do you live near campus?"

David began to squirm in his seat. He couldn't take Arch to his fraternity house, because Arch wasn't a member and because he "wouldn't fit in." He noticed Arch's inexpensive jeans and shirt and knew they would have to meet elsewhere.

"Well, I do live near campus," David admitted and named the fraternity to which he belonged.

"I see." Arch understood at once. "You could come to my house. I live at home, but it's quite far away. We'd have to take a bus."

"That's fine," David agreed. "I'd like to meet your family. But we can take my car. My parents bought me a little Porsche for my birthday last month. It'll fit us and our heavy chemistry books." He laughed self-consciously.

"All right. I'll meet you in front of the student union at five. I have to go to another class now," Arch said, collecting his books.

At five o'clock David drove up in his shiny black Porsche. Arch made no remark about the car and began to give David directions to his home.

As they drove on, the neighborhoods became poorer and poorer. They finally pulled up in front of a small white house with a tiny porch.

Arch opened the unlocked door and motioned David inside. His mother came out of the kitchen, wearing an apron.

"Hello, David," she greeted him heartily, "Arch told me he'd be bringing a friend to dinner. I'm so glad you could come."

David was overwhelmed by the greeting. Arch hadn't mentioned dinner! The house smelled wonderful with the food cooking, and a tiny fireplace was lit.

The dining room table wore an old, but clean, white tablecloth, and it was set for three.

"Isn't your dad coming? Does he have to work late?" David asked.

"No." Arch's voice was low and serious. "He died two years ago. Heart attack. He worked two jobs to keep the family together, and it proved to be too much."

"How do you manage tuition for college?" David was shocked.

"He has a scholarship — a full scholarship because he was an A student in high school." Arch's mother walked in carrying a platter.

"Let me help," Arch jumped up. "You've worked all day."

She gratefully accepted his help and went back to the kitchen for more food.

At last they sat down to eat. The conversation was easy and the food delicious. The house felt cozy to David. He couldn't remember a time when a dinner had been so peaceful.

"Thank you," he said when they had finished their dessert.

"Let's hurry and do the dishes before we study," Arch urged David.

It was a new experience for David. He dried dishes for the first time in his life and found he enjoyed it.

Afterward the boys studied, and Arch proved to be an excellent tutor. David understood the work much better.

Over the next few months David and Arch became fast friends. They had many conversations in the little white house about life and their ambitions.

One day David was confronted by one of his fraternity brothers.

"We see you prefer certain students on campus who aren't members of our frat," he accused. "This is only your first year in the house. Perhaps you're not comfortable with us."

"Not at all," David answered, "but I would like to bring Arch over for dinner. I've been at his home countless times."

"You know the rules," he was told. "You belong here with us. You swore at your initiation to be loyal to the group."

David went to his room and sat in an easy chair next to a window overlooking the campus.

It is pretty here, he thought, but the beauty in Arch's house cannot be discounted.

He knew that to remain a fraternity brother in good standing he would have to give up his friendship with Arch. At least, he couldn't see him as often.

Arch had proved himself a real friend.

David could always leave the fraternity and move to a dormitory.

Where should his loyalties lie? He sat until dusk thinking about the question.

- If you had been David, what would your decision have been?

CHAPTER 8

Loyalty in Friendship

Friends do not always come in twos, even though you hear, "She is my best friend," or, "I've know him since first grade; we've been buddies over since."

Friends often come in groups of five, six, or more. They spend most of their time together playing, studying, confiding in one another. Frequently they become so close that they are almost a second family.

They tell each other about their successes and worries, about grades, family life, and boyfriend or girlfriend troubles. They know each other, trust each other, enjoy each other — they are friends.

Sometimes, however, the ugly head of gossip rears itself when one member of the group is not around.

Let's look at one such time.

Suzanne's Slumber Party

Suzanne's birthday was on Saturday. Her mother and father had agreed to allow her to have a slumber party with her group of five friends. There was Beth, who was in all of Suzanne's classes at junior high school; Mary, who was in her dance class; Gail, who lived next door; Lisa, from her study group; and Patty, who had moved into the neighborhood the year before.

It was amazing to Suzanne's mother how well the girls got along. She heard them talking and laughing, whispering their secrets to each other, and she watched them get closer and closer. She was proud of Suzanne's ability to make friends, and she determined to help make the party a success by preparing the girl's favorite foods and topping the night off with a huge birthday cake. Suzanne's name would be in the middle, and her friends' names would form a circle around the birthday girl.

As the time for the party approached, Suzanne was excited.

Suddenly the phone rang. It was Gail. Her voice sounded strange and hoarse.

"Suzanne, I'm sorry I can't come to your party," she explained between coughs. "I have a fever and a sore throat."

"But you can't miss tonight!" Suzanne was upset. "Can't you take an aspirin and feel better?"

"I've already tried that, but Mother is taking me to the doctor because my fever is kinda high."

"We'll miss you, but we'll save you some cake," Suzanne answered. "Get better!"

Before she could get all upset, the doorbell rang and Lisa came in with her sleeping bag and a present. The bell rang again, and Mary came in, wearing tights and carrying a present.

"I like to sleep in my dance clothes," she laughed, "then I dream about being a ballerina."

In a few minutes all the girls were assembled and seated on the floor of the cleared living room.

Variously colored sleeping bags and outfits made a colorful splash.

Suzanne's mother came in bearing trays of food and warned the girls of a surprise at ten o'clock.

Patty, in her bunny pajamas, began to tell jokes about her last school before moving into the neighborhood, and everybody was in stitches.

"Wait a minute," Lisa interrupted. "Where is Gail?"

"Sick, sore throat, fever," Suzanne answered, her mouth full of potato chips.

"Can't say I miss her," Lisa said.

There was a moment's silence. The girls felt uncomfortable.

Patty said, "But Gail isn't here to defend herself."

Lisa was relentless. "She wouldn't defend herself if she could." Her tone was nasty.

"What's that supposed to mean?" Suzanne asked, suddenly annoyed.

"She is such a mouse. I believe that's what Lisa meant," Beth said. "She's part of our group just because she lives next door and you've known her since you were babies. But she is a big bore."

"What has she ever done to you?" Suzanne was incredulous.

Lisa and Patty laughed. "Nothing, absolutely nothing. That's the problem. She's a hanger-on to give herself status, that's all."

"And her hair," Beth added nastily. "I'm frankly embarrassed to be seen with her. She wears it like a little girl."

"Yes, I bet her mommy still combs it," Patty added.

No one had noticed that Suzanne had slipped out of the room.

She found her mother in an upstairs bedroom.

"Mother," she said, "I want everyone to go home."

"Your friends?" Suzanne's mother was surprised. "They came to celebrate. Don't be rude."

"Mother, they're no one's friends. They've been making fun of Gail all evening. Gail has been my friend forever. I can't let them talk like that."

"Do you need my help in asking the girls to leave?" Her mother understood.

"You can call their parents and ask them to pick them up."

"All right, dear, but remember it'll be hard on you when you go back to school on Monday."

"I know," Suzanne said quietly, "it's hard already."

She returned to the living room and announced, "Party's over. Your parents are coming to get you."

"Are you kidding?" Lisa said, "You have a strange sense of humor."

"I'm not being funny," the birthday girl answered, "just loyal to my friend, Gail. I can't allow you to talk about her in the gossipy way you did."

"Gossip isn't being disloyal," Patty snapped. "If you hadn't been in the group, we probably would have talked about you. It doesn't mean a thing."

"I'm sorry," Suzanne answered, "it means everything to me. We're either friends or we're not."

"Well, then, I guess we aren't." Lisa's high-pitched voice carried over the protests of the others. "A little harmless gossip, and you get all riled up."

But the girls gathered their sleeping bags.

"Please take your presents," Suzanne asked.

"Okey-dokey," Patty said. "I wanted it for myself anyway."

"Thanks for the party," Beth said huffily as she left to wait for her parents' car.

After everyone was gone, Suzanne's mother came downstairs.

"I'm so proud of you, young lady. You are a real friend to Gail."

They went into the kitchen where the ten o'clock surprise cake was.

Suzanne took a knife and expertly refrosted the top of the cake, wiping out the girls' names and leaving only Gail and herself.

"Mother, may I take the cake next door?" Suzanne asked.

"But Gail is sick." The protest came swiftly.

"I'll only be a minute."

Her mother nodded agreement.

Suzanne knocked on Gail's door, cake in hand. Gail answered in a bathrobe, surprised to see her friend.

"What are you doing here?" she croaked in her funny sore-throat voice.

"Just sharing my cake with my sick friend," Suzanne answered. They stuck their fingers in the icing, then Gail's mother came.

"Off to bed, Gail!" she commanded. She turned to Suzanne. "You are a wonderful friend, dear. I'll freeze the cake and you girls can have it when Gail is better."

The croaky voice of Gail came from the bedroom. "I have a

"I'm sure he is," Ann replied, "but I've hiked up here before. It's sad, but many people drop their dogs off here when they no longer want them."

"I can't believe it," Margaret cried. "We must take the dog with us and find a home."

"He doesn't look as though he could make it as far as the car."

"Then let's carry him," Margaret said unrealistically.

A young couple sat a few yards away from the girls, also having a picnic. They, too, had noticed the dog.

After a few moments they came over to the girls.

"May we give your dog the rest of our picnic?" they asked.

"He's not ours. He's lost," Margaret said, beginning to cry.

The couple began to feed the dog. He ate every bit they gave him, and his tail began to wag.

"Honey," the young woman asked her husband, "how do you feel about taking him home?"

The man winked at the girls. "Only if I can name him Humphrey," he laughed.

The dog seemed to understand. Everyone cleaned up after their lunches and set out toward their cars.

"Come, Humphrey, come," they took turns shouting. Humphrey trotted happily along. Occasionally he flopped down, and the group waited until he was rested.

Humphrey made it down the mountainside.

"Come, Humphrey," the young husband shouted as he opened his car door.

Humphrey climbed into the back seat. His new mistress sat in front and waved at the girls.

Humphrey had found a loyal couple to care for him at last.

When you beg your parents for a pet, remember that you must be dependable and loyal to the animal. It is a living being, not a toy to be tossed away when you tire of it.

- Had you been on the mountain picnic and seen the dog, how willing would you have been to consider possible solutions?
- How willing are you to look for ways in which you personally can do something about seemingly impossible situations?

CHAPTER 9

Loyalty in Jobs and Communities

The TV show "L. A. Law" had an episode in which one of the lawyers in a large firm decided to give the secretaries (about ten, in all), staggered lunch hours. Because they would all go out at slightly different times, they would not be able to have lunch together, as they used to.

The secretaries were very angry and demanded to know the reason. The lawyer said that he wanted the office "covered" at all times.

At first that made sense, but soon the secretaries realized that they were not trusted. The lawyer wanted complete control over them and acted as though he might have been cheated of their time. He had never caught anyone coming in late after lunch, but he assumed that they might do so — if not now, then sometime in the future.

Moreover, the secretaries wanted and deserved a raise but were told the firm couldn't afford it.

One day the secretaries met secretly and decided to walk out. Surely, they thought, the lawyer who was in charge of them would ask them to return. One of the secretaries was afraid, however, afraid she might lose her job.

And that is what happened. All ten women were fired.

One of the secretaries talked with another lawyer of the firm. "What can we do?" she wailed.

"You might have listened when you were told there was no money for a raise," the second lawyer responded. "None of us lawyers are getting raises this year, either. But I believe you deserve your lunch hour back. There was no reason not to trust all of you. We know you put in a full day's work every day."

The spokeswoman for the other secretaries marched into the first lawyer's office. He asked her to sit down.

"I'm afraid we haven't been very loyal," she offered. "We didn't realize you couldn't afford to give us a raise."

"I wish I could," he answered and smiled for the first time.

"We're ready to come back to work if you still want us," she said.

"Of course, we want you," he responded.

"However, we must have your respect. You cannot treat us like children. We know when to go out for lunch and when to return. You know, loyalty is a two-way street."

The lawyer looked at her long and hard. Finally he got up. The secretary also stood. The lawyer extended his hand and said simply, "You've got your lunch hour any way you want it. And you have all of my respect and loyalty."

- Loyalty is a two-way street. What does that mean?
- Why did the secretaries feel that their boss was not loyal to them?

On a job, loyalty between worker and boss is important if the company is to run smoothly. Everyone is much happier if he is trusted. If a worker is appreciated and trusted, he usually does much more than is expected of him.

Loyalty for one another brings people face to face with a greater sense of equality — and that always makes for greater harmony.

Volunteers serve Thanksgiving dinners to homeless people in Washington. It is one way of showing care and concern for needy members of their community.

Loyalty in Our Communities

Have you ever heard people complain, "No one cares about anyone else any more! I don't even know my neighbors."

Sadly, that is often the case in our large cities. However, circumstances can change it in a few moments.

When disaster strikes, such as an earthquake, a tornado, or war, people go out of their way to help each other. The neighbor whose name you never knew may help you with her first aid kit or bring you something to eat. People need people, especially in times of stress.

It is wonderful when something good develops out of a horrible time, but what about everyday loyalty to our communities? Is that possible?

In many cities all over the United States, a new program called "Save a Block" has begun. Neighbors walk around with large garbage bags to pick up litter and clean the street. In other neighborhoods, people have gotten together to paint an apartment house to give a fresh look to their block.

More important, neighbors have gotten together with experts on child care and started cooperative nursery schools. Mothers take turns teaching and caring for groups of very young children.

In some communities tutoring programs have begun because people realize the importance of reading and learning.

All these examples show loyalty to communities. Communities can be made better and more fun to live in if everyone does his share. There are talents that no one knows about in any given community.

If you have a community center, go there sometime and see how you can fit in and how you can be of service.

Sometimes a sign of being loyal to your community is simply helping a child who is not sure of himself to cross the street or carrying a grocery bag for an elderly person. You'll be handsomely rewarded: You'll feel good and probably get a big smile from a lonely person.

Loyalty to your community makes life more pleasant for everyone. Imagine, if everyone cared, no one would be afraid to walk on the street at night or fear being robbed.

A high school student helps a physically impaired boy from a neighboring school identify different foods in the kitchen.

Again, trust is the aspect that comes about when loyalty is in the community.

- Is loyalty a necessary value in our community?
- What happens if no one is loyal to his neighbors?
- In what ways do we need each other?

CHAPTER 10

How Loyalty Affects Our Nation

You have probably read about the lives of our nation's heroes. These people proved their loyalty by putting the good of others above the good of self.

What does that mean? It means that when a decision had to be made about who would benefit from an action, the loyal person put others ahead of himself or herself.

During the Revolutionary War soldiers fought against terrible odds. They sacrificed themselves so that America could be freed from British rule. They put a new nation ahead of their own lives. Today we have the United States, a free country. We can thank the soldiers of the Revolutionary War.

You don't have to be famous to be loyal to your country. You do need to be a good citizen, and you do need to be ready to help in the best way you can when help is required.

Loyalty to Country Is Also a Two-way Street

That does not mean that you have to follow the leaders of the nation blindly and believe everything you hear on the news. On the contrary! You must sift the information you get daily and decide what is the best course of action for you and your country.

When you are old enough you express your wishes in a voting booth and elect people to represent you in Washington, DC, or in your state capital, or at city hall. You yourself might become a representative, and it will be your duty to help the people you represent. Again, you will find that loyalty is a two-way street.

Many years ago, Mark Twain wrote something important about patriotism and loyalty to one's country. In his book *A Connecticutt Yankee in King Arthur's Court*, Twain said:

> "Loyalty to government has never been my idea of patriotism. The country is the real thing, the lasting thing. Institutions of government are merely the clothing which the nation wears; and clothing can be worn out, used up, in need of mending or repair.
>
> Governments are rags. To be loyal to rags, to shout for rags, to worship rags, is to ignore the health of the body that wears the clothing. This not true loyalty to one's country."

What does that mean? It means that to show loyalty to your country you do not have to follow in footsteps that may no longer be of any use. If someone tells you, "But we've always done it this way," that is no reason to continue doing it that way. There is always room for change, provided the change is made for the greatest good of as many as possible.

When you pledge allegiance to the flag, you are really promising loyalty to your country — a country that has given you freedom of choice.

- How can you express loyalty to the nation?
- Why is loyalty a needed value to keep our country whole and safe?
- If you could make a law that would benefit many people in this country, what would it be?

Loyalty: A Lifelong Concern

Your experience with loyalty will go on throughout your life. But whatever your experience is, you have to begin where you are, to start your journey of self-discovery there.

An old story illustrates the futility of trying to start from anywhere else:

A man is lost in the country roads of Vermont, and he stops at a field to ask directions of a farmer.

"How can I get to New York?"

The farmer chews on his grass stem thoughtfully for a while, and then he says, "Mister, if I was you, I wouldn't start from here!"

No matter how inexperienced, confused, and lost you are about the place of dependability and loyalty in your life, you have to start from here. It may be a hard place to start, but there is no alternative. It is the only place to start. You can be proud of yourself for taking the journey.

PART THREE

Loyalty and History

Throughout history, stories of heroes and heroines who were loyal to their country or to an idea have shown us the courage it takes to be loyal.

These heroes have also helped us understand what causes and ideas we should be loyal to.

CHAPTER 11

Historical Perspectives

Norman Thomas in his book *Great Dissenters* wrote, "The secret of a good life is to have the right loyalties and hold them in the right scale of values."

He meant that you must hold on to your true beliefs. If others think differently and try to change your values, and you go back and forth losing your choice of the truth, you are not leading a happy or a good life.

You realize where your values lie. We live in a free society, and loyalty is a positive part of us. If others compete with our loyalties, it can disrupt our society.

Over the centuries loyalties have widened from the family to the tribe, the village, the city, and finally the nation. In modern times some people go beyond the nation and want world government. They feel loyalty to everyone in the world.

As you are beginning to see, loyalty is of many kinds. When a choice has to be made between loyalty to opposite ideas, your conscience is your best guide. You have also been brought up a certain way, and that can influence your behavior as you decide on your set of values.

There was a time when loyalty was demanded of people. In Europe during the fifteenth and sixteenth centuries, small states existed. Each state expected the loyalty of its people.

The states were run by feudal lords, who owned huge lands. The people who worked for them, called serfs, were practically slaves. The serfs had to be completely obedient and loyal to their lords or suffer severe punishment.

- Is that true loyalty as you understand it?
- Can anyone demand loyalty?

By the eighteenth century things had changed, especially in America. Americans had to choose whether to be loyal to England, the mother country, or to the Colonies. In the Declaration of Independence a new kind of loyalty began. It was the idea of government by consent of the governed. You did not have to be loyal if you did not agree.

- What is the difference between loyalty in the days of the feudal lords and loyalty as described in the Declaration of Independence?

Thomas Jefferson wrote, "Resistance to tyrants is obedience to God."

It was wonderful to have a government under which the people could decide to agree or to disagree. They had a choice about where to place their loyalty.

From time to time, however, in years to come, even this government began to question the loyalty of various groups of people.

One such time came about in 1950. The US Congress had passed the Internal Security Act, which stated that certain citizens were disloyal to the United States.

Investigations were made of government workers, movie stars, and college professors. People felt like strangers to each other. They became lonely and fearful. A demand was made that citizens taken an oath of loyalty to the United States. That was just the opposite of the basic values of a government by consent.

Later the investigations of government workers showed that 98 percent of those accused of disloyalty were innocent. Finally, the loyalty oath was dismissed.

- Which idea most appeals to you: Jefferson's resistance to tyrants, or being forced to show loyalty by taking an oath?
- Which of the two ideas would make people truly loyal to their country?

In a democracy, loyalty has to be given freely. Only then is it meaningful.

The American philosopher Josiah Royce wrote, "He who is truly free is truly loyal."

CHAPTER 12

Some Commandments as Guidelines

"Honor thy father and thy mother" is the Fifth Commandment in the Bible. Even thousands of years ago, the question of loyalty was there.

What does this Commandment mean? Again, as in all aspects of loyalty, you have to decide.

Some think it means that you have to be obedient to your parents at all times.

You may ask, "Does that mean that my parents are always right, and because they are right their decisions are good and just?"

Some think the Fifth Commandment means that you can never be equal with your parents, but must put them in a place of honor, a place higher than yours.

Let's explore some other ways to look at this Commandment.

Your parents are human. They love you, but they make mistakes as all humans do. Does that mean we cannot honor them?

Let's substitute the word "accept" for honor.

If you don't judge your parents, but simply accept them as they are, you are showing great respect and — loyalty.

Gabby's Alcoholic Father

Gabby lived with her father in a small apartment in Chicago. She was seventeen years old.

Her mother had died in a car accident when Gabby was only ten. From the day of the funeral, her father had begun to drink.

At first he seemed relaxed and jolly when he drank, but as the years passed he consumed more and more liquor. The more he drank, the angrier he became. Sometimes the anger expressed itself in silent moodiness. At other times he shouted at Gabby. She knew the neighbors could hear every word, and she was embarrassed.

However, no matter how angry and drunk her father became, Gabby never judged him. When friends asked, "How can you stand it?" she never spoke against her father. She did show concern. She often cried in frustration and hurt, but she understood her father's loneliness.

Finally, in her teen years, she received counseling from Al-Anon, an organization to help relatives of alcoholics.

- How did Gabby deal with the Fifth Commandment?
- Does an accepting attitude show itself in loyalty? How?

When you love your parents, they experience great joy and satisfaction. This is still another way of "honoring." Honor, love, respect, understanding, and loyalty all fit together in the Fifth Commandment.

Forgiveness as a Part of Loyalty

One more aspect of loyalty to your parents is forgiveness.

Some people carry a grudge against their mother and father that may last into adulthood and even old age when the parents are dead.

It can come from not having been loved enough or having been mistreated in some way. If that is something you feel is happening to you, you need to let your parents know. Carrying a grudge is a burden. It is not good for you or for them.

Try talking it out with your parents. If that doesn't work, ask for help from a responsible adult. Your parents might get help, and that is a form of loyalty to them.

Above all, try to understand why they act as they do. Understanding leads to forgiveness. If you have been mistreated you may not want to be close to your mother or father, but you can try to forgive them. They made a serious mistake, but it is not your fault.

In forgiving them, you honor them and show loyalty of the highest kind.

- How do you show loyalty to your mother and father?
- How did you decide to use the word "honor," as used in the Fifth Commandment?
- Why are love and forgiveness important aspects of loyalty?

Thou Shalt Not Steal

One of the most basic ways you can show loyalty to others is to recognize their possessions, to obey the Eighth Commandment.

You may say, "Of course, I wouldn't steal. My friend's bike or my friend's car are off limits. I know the difference between right and wrong."

Most people are like you. The mere thought of taking something from another person — stealing — is repulsive.

Yet every day cars are stolen, homes are broken into, purses are snatched off women's shoulders. Not everyone who steals is a professional thief.

Many people steal to support a drug habit. The question is, "Is the thief primarily out to steal money or does he need drugs?" Which came first? Drugs or stealing? How can we help?

We can all pull together to recognize a boy or girl who may be about to use drugs. Teachers, friends, parents all need to be on the alert for the young person who does not feel good about himself or herself. Often the problem arises when families don't work well together. There are fights and arguments at home and the son or daughter turns to drugs for comfort, then to stealing.

A boy or girl may be having trouble at school. Instead of

moving a little more slowly, he or she may feel stupid or a failure and turn to drugs, which give a false picture of himself or herself.

Not all stealing is drug-related, as you know, but we need to give real values to everyone in our society, including those on drugs.

We need to praise others for the things they can do, and not focus on things they cannot do. We need to recognize them for what they are. When we gossip, or blame others, or make fun of them, we are really stealing a part of them.

"Thou shalt not steal" goes much further than taking things away from each other.

The Orchestra

Jan always wanted to play the flute, but her parents could not afford one. When she was in sixth grade, a teacher gave Jan a flute she had had when she was a child.

Jan was thrilled and taught herself to play. By the time she went to junior high school, she felt confident enough to try out for the orchestra. The music teacher realized that Jan's playing was pretty rough, but her enthusiasm and willingness to practice helped the teacher decide to let her join.

At the first rehearsal Jan realized that she was outclassed. Everyone had had private lessons, and most of the students read music easily. Jan was slow. She flushed with the effort to keep up. At the end of the hour she asked permission to take the score home. She determined to practice until she was as good as the others.

Her constant practicing began to annoy her mother.

"You give me a headache," she would scream. "Stop that noise!"

Jan could find no place to practice and began to feel very frustrated. Still, she tried her best.

At a rehearsal of the orchestra, just before the first concert, a student jumped up and said, "Mr. Cross, I can't play when Jan sits next to me. She makes so many mistakes."

"Yeah, she's ruining our concert," another student piped up. "Why doesn't she take more lessons?"

A few more members joined in the complaints. Despite Mr. Cross's attempts to intervene, Jan dropped out of the orchestra. She didn't want the disapproval of everyone.

- What was stolen from Jan?
- How did Jan's mother contribute to the theft?
- How could Jan regain what was stolen from her?
- Could the orchestra members have shown loyalty to Jan? How?

Are Cheating and Stealing the Same Thing?

Have you ever taken a test and known the answer to a question — but were not too sure of yourself? Did you look at your neighbor's paper to confirm your answer?

You may argue that you knew the answer and just wanted to check it out. That is true. But a greater truth is relying on yourself, taking the honorable way, and risking being wrong.

If your answers were correct — great! If your answers were incorrect and you risked that possibility, you have the value of loyalty to yourself on your side. Chances are that you'll never remember the question on that test when you grow up, but you might recall that you valued the truth, even as a young adult.

People cheat in many ways. A saleswoman who tells a customer that she looks beautiful in a certain outfit (and the customer looks terrible) is cheating.

A child splitting a candy bar with a friend and taking the larger piece for herself is cheating.

A car salesman changing the price of a car and telling his customer he's "getting a great deal" is cheating.

A politician promising improvements and not carrying through after election is cheating.

A baby-sitter talking on the phone all evening, leaving a small child unattended, is cheating.

A newspaper carrying a sensational story that is only partly true is cheating.

What is taken away in each instance?

If something is taken away without permission, it is stealing.

Can you see the connection between cheating and stealing?

Loyalty to others cannot involve cheating.

Stealing from the Rich to Give to the Poor

Ever since Robin Hood, people have wondered whether "stealing from the rich to give to the poor" is not really stealing.

The question makes us uncomfortable because we don't want to see our fellowman cold and hungry. It is one of the gray areas we discussed in an earlier chapter.

Robin Hood's story involved loyalty and honor.

During the Middle Ages, England was divided into two classes: noblemen and serfs. The noblemen had all the land and riches, while the serfs worked like slaves for them.

Richard was the King of England, and like many nobles of his time, he decided to fight in the Crusades. On his journey, King Richard was kidnapped and taken hostage. The kidnappers demanded a huge ransom.

While the King was in captivity many noblemen betrayed him. His own brother took over the throne. When Prince John betrayed Richard, many noblemen had to make a choice. Should they support John and ask his help? Or should they wait for the return of the rightful King to the throne?

Most were disloyal.

One nobleman, Sir Robin of Locksley, remained loyal to King Richard. He started guerrilla warfare against Prince John.

Meanwhile, the noblemen continued to abuse the serfs. They taxed them so heavily that the serfs practically had no life other than work and hunger.

Sir Robin was on the side of the poor, and with his band of men faithful to King Richard he stole from the noblemen and gave to the serfs. Soon Sir Robin came to be called Robin Hood.

Finally, according to the legend, Robin Hood managed to take enough tax money from the noblemen to pay the ransom to the kidnappers, and King Richard was freed.

- Do you agree with Robin Hood's way of helping the poor?
- In what ways did the noblemen show their disloyalty?
- The noblemen forced the serfs to pay almost all they owned as taxes. Was that a form of stealing?

Alternatives

These are no longer the Middle Ages. What alternatives to stealing can we use to help each other and retain loyalty not only to ourselves but to our community?

One way we can overcome poverty is through the use of economics.

Gandhi's Cottage Industries

For many years England ruled the great country of India. India lost much of its wealth to England, and the people were heavily taxed.

Beggars roamed the streets. Sick and hungry children, with little or no clothing, cried in their mother's arms. Entire families lived in one-room "apartments" in the large cities.

The farmers grew cotton, which was shipped to England to be made into cloth. Then the Indians had to buy the cloth back, paying heavy taxes on the cotton they had grown.

The rich were getting richer and, as you might guess, the poor were getting poorer.

Fortunately a new leader got the people's attention. His name was Mohandas Gandhi. He wanted a better life for his people, especially the poor. And he wanted independence from England.

How could this be accomplished? Gandhi had an idea: The Indians would no longer buy the cotton cloth from England. However, they needed the cool cotton for clothes in the hot Indian climate.

Gandhi told the people to keep the cotton they had grown, and he started "cottage industries." People worked in their homes to produce what England's big factories had produced before.

The Indian people spun thread to be made into cloth by using a simple spinning wheel. All over the country, people sat and spun thread. Even Gandhi, their leader, spun for many hours a day.

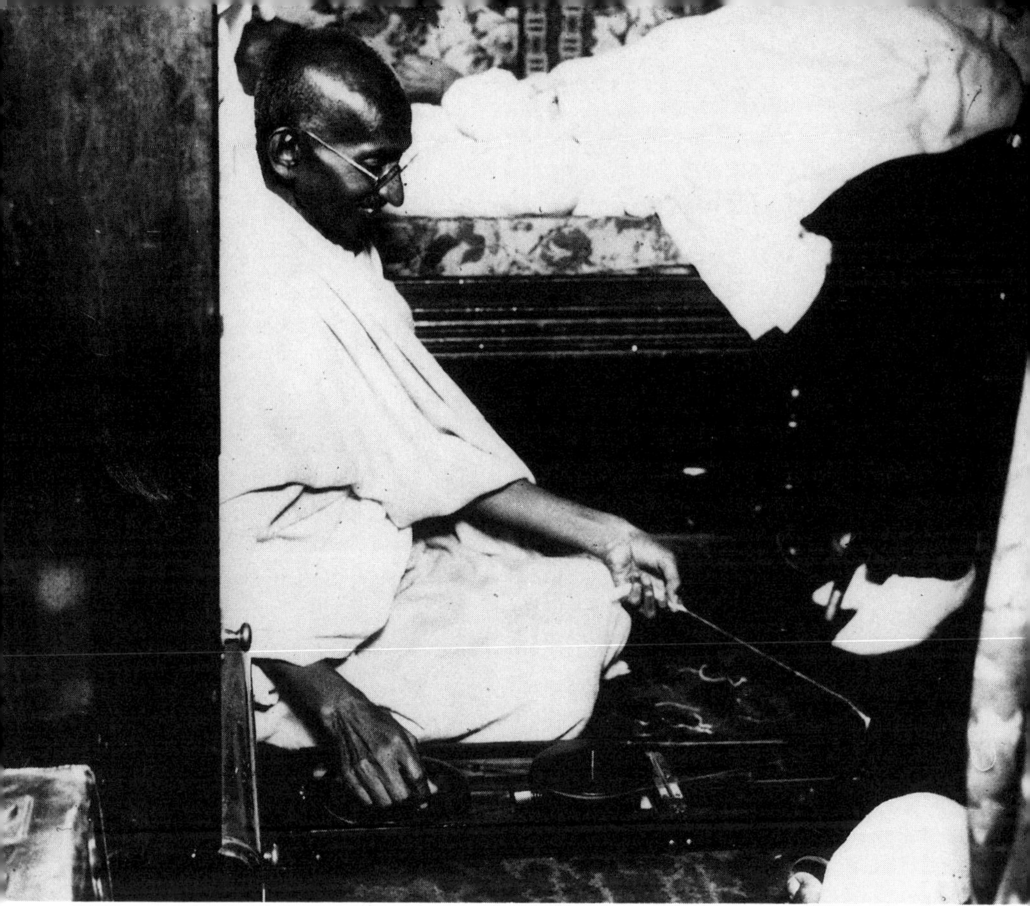

Gandhi urged the Indian people to follow his example and spin their own cotton thread.

The English were furious. They had made money with cotton, and now the poor people had taken back their rightful goods from the rich.

Gandhi did this in a quiet, peaceful way. He was loyal to the poor, and his plan worked.

Much later, India became independent because of Gandhi's plans.

- By not supporting the rich, what had Gandhi gained?
- Did Gandhi have to steal?

Change through Peaceful Means

Martin Luther King was another man who helped the poor and yet remained loyal to his country, the United States.

Dr. King saw how black people suffered in the South. They were not only poor but treated as though they were inferior. They were not allowed to drink from the same water fountains as whites. They were not permitted to go to school with white children. In some states blacks were not allowed to vote. The list of injustices was long.

But the worst part was the poverty and fear in which black people lived.

Dr. King decided to help. He got his people together and marched arm-in-arm with them to Washington to ask for the right to a dignified life.

He did not help only blacks, but whites and other minorities as well. Soon all sorts of people all over the country joined Martin Luther King's marches, listened to his speeches, and helped him to bring about change.

Today, as you know, people of all races and creeds can live where they want, drink from any water fountain, go to any school they choose, and work at any job for which they are qualified.

Dr. King was loyal not only to his people, but to all people who were poor and needed help.

He did not steal. He, like Gandhi, brought about change through peaceful means. He appealed to the conscience of people, and they responded.

- How many ways can you think of to replace stealing with honor, loyalty, and hard work?
- "Thou shalt not steal" is an old Commandment. Does it still have value for you?

Dr. Martin Luther King stands arm-in-arm with supporters at the graveside of a demonstrator.

CHAPTER 13

Thou Shalt Not Kill

"Thou shalt not kill" is the sixth of the Ten Commandments. Although you view killing and murder daily on your TV screen, take a moment to think, to feel, to absorb the absolute horror of taking life from another human being. It is a taking that is forever. The murdered person will not come back.

Killing is a disloyal act against mankind. Imagine the proud parents of a newborn infant experiencing the miracle of life. A few years later the infant now grown into teenager is dead, murdered. Taken from his parents forever. Taken from his friends. Taken from life itself.

"Thou shalt not kill" means to respect life and not take it lightly or for granted. Loving life and giving to it is loyalty.

Killing is a permanent theft. It never solves a problem — it simply creates more problems for more people.

The Tragedy of Macbeth

Four hundred years ago Shakespeare wrote the play *Macbeth*, which deals with the feelings of a murderer. Still performed, it is a story of disloyalty, murder, and guilt. The feelings written about are the same today.

Macbeth and his wife committed murder to get what they thought they wanted from life. They wanted power and glory, and to get their wish they killed the King of Scotland.

The King trusted Macbeth, and when Macbeth approached his bed one night to murder him, he violated his loyalty to his country and to his leader.

Although Macbeth and his wife became King and Queen of Scotland, they created confusion in the land they thought they could rule. They destroyed what had been beautiful and noble in themselves. Terrible guilt shook them both.

In truth, part of Macbeth had not wanted to murder the King. When he did, after much thinking, it was because his ambition ruled him. His conscience and sense of loyalty fell away from him. He became obsessed with wanting more and more for himself.

At the end of the play, everyone realizes that the true Macbeth was a pitiful creature with "the mind of a great man turned criminal."

Macbeth's wife, who had been his accomplice, became Queen, but she went insane with her self-inflicted tortures of guilt.

Before Macbeth and his wife died, their consciences constantly troubled them, and they were "walking shadows" — people no longer in control of themselves, no longer in touch with reality.

Thou shalt not kill!

- Do you think the Commandment is a simple one to follow?
- Can it enter the "gray areas" we discussed in Chapter 4?

Killing during Wartime

During wartime, ordinary citizens are drafted into the armed services; that is, they are ordered by the government to become soldiers to defend the country. Some people go to war voluntarily; that is called enlisting.

Many go to war and come back heroes. Heroes who kept women and children safe, who put themselves in grave danger to help their fellow soldiers, who did their best in battle to defeat the enemy.

I WAS THERE
AND
PROUD OF IT

A hero who comes back from war has shown loyalty to his country. He had to defend the freedom of his land.

How would you feel if another country tried to take our freedom away by conquering the United States? Wouldn't you admire the loyalty, bravery, and courage of the soldiers who went to battle and risked their lives for you?

- Can killing be an act of loyalty if it is done in self-defense or in defense of your country?
- What is the difference between the kind of killing done by Macbeth and that done by a soldier whose land has been attacked?

Pacifists

Some people believe so completely in peace that even if their country is attacked, they refuse to go to war. They would prefer to be killed than to kill. They are called pacifists.

How do they show loyalty to their country? Many pacifists during wartime help in peaceful ways. They may fill positions left by those who became soldiers. They may become teachers, nurses, or even go to the battlefield to help the wounded, but they refuse to pick up a gun or to shoot the enemy.

They believe they are loyal not only to their own country, but to the world. Their argument is that if no one becomes a soldier, there could not be a war. Do you think we could ever live in such a world?

Jains

In India there is a group of pacifists called the Jains. Their loyalty is not only to human beings, but to all creatures on earth. They feel that all that live have equal rights to existence.

Two Vietnam veterans remember the loyalty and courage of their friends who died in battle.

Jains are vegetarians. They eat neither meat, eggs, nor fish. They don't kill mosquitoes, flies, or snakes. They let all creatures be, no matter how uncomfortable they may feel with an insect or a worm crawling on them.

Theirs is a profound belief and loyalty in the dignity of life. Jains consider it a great sin to kill.

- What is your position on pacifism?
- What are its advantages or drawbacks?
- How do you interpret the Commandment, "Thou shalt not kill?"

Once again, you have to struggle with a concept: "Thou shalt not kill." It is the big struggle for the conscience of mankind.

The questions relating to this Commandment present themselves in many forms in our complex world.

You may want to think about some of them.

1. Are drug dealers potential murderers? Does the word "potential" make them killers?
2. Should doctors take hopelessly ill patients off of life-support systems? At what point in an illness can the doctor decide whether a person is "hopelessly" ill?
3. What is your belief about abortion?
4. How should drunken drivers be regarded?
5. Is it all right to wipe out whole species of animals for business purposes?
6. What can be done about oil spills that pollute our oceans and kill sea life?

- You can probably recall many other instances where unintentional killing takes place. What are some of them?
- As our planet "shrinks," who is responsible for life-preserving laws?

These questions require deep thought and reflection. Does the all-important value of loyalty to your world fit in with some of your answers?

PART FOUR

Heroes Whose Loyalty We Emulate

Throughout history, there have been exceptionally loyal people who were true to a cause to help others with little or no thought for themselves.

Some sacrificed their entire lives to their cause, others put themselves in danger; but all are remembered for their loyalty and fairness. They still serve as examples to all of us.

Hungry, scared, and parentless, this small victim of a natural disaster in India protects his body with a piece of torn cloth.

sometimes doubled back to confuse the pursuers. Harriet Tubman personally accompanied many frightened runaways and often was able to effect a reunion of families once they had reached freedom.

Hers is a story of loyalty not only to her people, but to the idea that each of us deserves freedom.

Harriet Tubman's loyalty and bravery will never be forgotten by people of all races.

- Loyalty is a value that can save others. Can you think of a story that would fit this idea?

Mother Theresa

You have seen how loyalty has had its impact on people of the past. Today we still have our heroes and heroines whose values we try to emulate.

One such heroine is Mother Theresa, a European nun who traveled to India. There she saw the unbelievable poverty of many people. Children wandered the streets half-naked, without parents, without food, and without shelter.

Others lay in the streets full of disease, begging for money to fill their rice bowls.

Many "worked" for beggar kings, who stole money from the poor each night in exchange for their life or a bowl of rice.

Mother Theresa saw families of twenty or more crowded into one or two rooms. She heard the wails of the sick. She decided to stay in Calcutta, one of India's largest cities, and try to help the needy.

Mother Theresa's loyalty was to anyone who needed her.

She began to treat the sick, providing a sanitary place so that infection would not continue to spread. She wore clothes like those of the people of India and lived in poverty herself.

Mother Theresa worked almost around the clock in her efforts to heal. She seldom rested, although she was no longer young.

She became world-famous because of her loyalty to the sick of India.

Mother Theresa was invited to speak about her work in

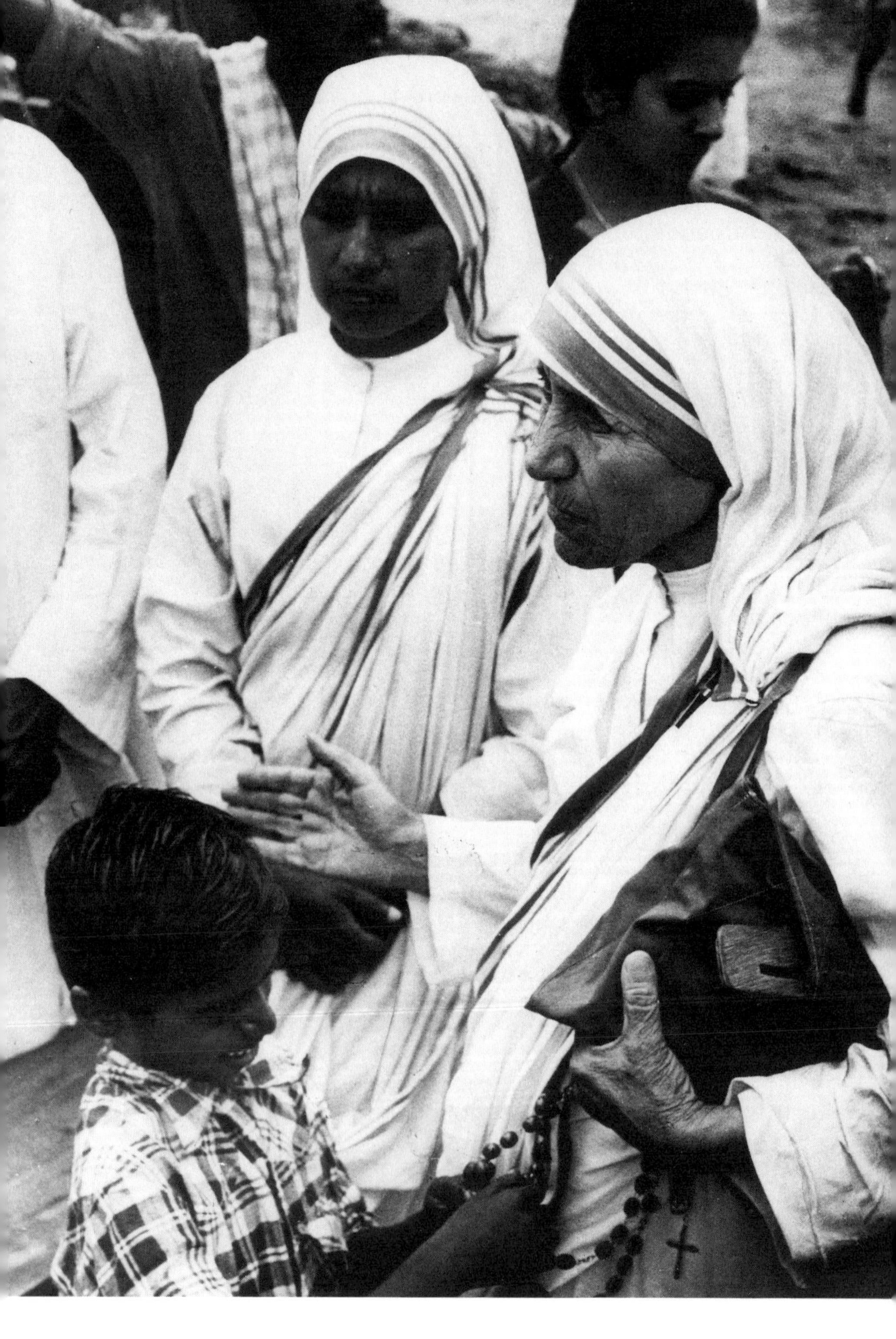

various countries. All she asked for was help for the sick she served — medical supplies, money for decent food. She asked nothing for herself.

Suddenly she became ill. It was no wonder, others said. Mother Theresa needed rest. Her own life was now at risk. Just as everyone had given up and thought she might die, she rallied, got a bit better, and continued her work. Finally, however, in 1990 she was unable to continue and had to retire.

- Why is Mother Theresa a heroine?
- Why do you think her awards are not important to her?
- Does the value of loyalty fit in with Mother Theresa's work? Explain.
- Some people thought she had no business in India. Yet she stayed. To whom did she really listen?

Joe de La Cruz

One of America's heroes we seldom hear about is Joe de La Cruz. He is alive and working for his cause today. His loyalty to his people has given him the respect of all who deal with him.

Joe de La Cruz became paramount chief of all the tribes of the Indian nations in America.

He belongs to the Quinault tribe, and his people are aware that he is mentioned with respect in Congress as well as in the White House.

De La Cruz is leading his people toward a goal — to regain their independence, their wealth, and, above all, their dignity.

Instead of fighting, as the old warrior chiefs did, he uses words and law books.

He does not use spears, but he has seen to it that there are land-preservation and wilderness regulations.

You know that the only true native American is the Indian.

Mother Theresa consoles a deaf-mute child. She has come to supervise relief operations in the village of Mandapahala, India, which has been devastated by a cyclone and tidal wave.

For 30,000 years or more Indians hunted, fished, and prayed in the mountains. Then the white man came and drove them into reservations.

Sadly, the American Indians have received hundreds of broken promises and dishonored treaties.

There are still one million Indians in the United States, but only half of them have left the reservations.

The Quinault reservation, from which Joe de La Cruz comes, is three hundred square miles, about the size of a small county in the United States. It is in the Pacific Northwest and was once a beautiful land.

The white men made a treaty in 1855 to protect it for the Indians. But over the years they herded other Indian tribes from the whole region into the reservation.

There is still a calm atmosphere on the reservation, even though it was used as a human dumping ground. The Indians have never gone hungry. There are salmon in the rivers and game in the forest.

The U.S. government gives the reservation $8 million a year, paid for by tax-paying Americans, but it is not enough. The Indians are still poor.

Did the Indians know what they were giving up long ago?

Joe de La Cruz says, "We all understood quite well that when our people signed the treaties and gave up vast areas of land in the Pacific Northwest, they were agreeing to live in a smaller area, a reservation. But we always thought we would be able to keep the rights that were written into those treaties; rights having to do with fishing, with the resources of the land, with the timber, with the game, and with the shorelines. The treaty also guaranteed we would be left in peace, that we would have control of our own destiny and the way we handled our life on the reservation."

He goes on to say that what he wants for his people is to rebuild what they have left. He wants the return of dignity for his tribe and all the other tribes.

When asked how he feels about himself as an Indian, he says, "I am first and foremost an Indian — and, secondly, an American. Even as a young child, it really was a very deep feeling. I always had it ingrained in me to be proud of my background, proud of my culture."

He has educated people who thought of Indians in terms of firewater, tomahawks, and war parties (ideas they probably got from movies). Indians are among the calmest of all people, he explains.

"You know, no matter what kind of conditions they are living in, they are still capable of being contented."

Because of his loyalty to his people, American national policy has come to think seriously about breaking up the reservations. He has set such a good example that hundreds of tribes are now also using the law and the courts to get back what was taken away.

Chief de La Cruz realizes there is still much to do and a long way to go to bring prosperity and good education to his people.

His grandfather warned him to be careful, not to become greedy or ambitious to gain victories. He advised him to be loyal to the Indian way, which means to protect only the basic things of Indian life — the fishing, the forest, the beach, the game, and the rivers.

What is Joe de La Cruz's hope?

"I believe," he says, "that America will one day look to us, as the first Americans, to take our place among them with pride and not lose our culture in the melting pot."

- Why is Chief de La Cruz a hero to his people?
- In what ways does he prove his loyalty as an Indian?

Golda Meir

Another twentieth-century heroine we can look up to and admire was Golda Meir.

She was born in the United States and was growing up at the time when Israel was becoming a nation. She was thrilled about the new country because any Jew could go there and call it home.

Throughout history, Jews have yearned for a land to call their own. They shuttled back and forth from one country to another because of prejudice against their religion and way of life.

Long ago they lived in Palestine, which Jews called the Promised Land. Even then, however, they encountered adversity with conquerors such as the Romans and others.

In Italy, Jews had to live in ghettos and were not permitted to mingle with the populace.

In Russia, the tsars who ruled for hundreds of years ordered "pogroms." Soldiers on horseback would overrun Jewish villages, destroying homes and killing the villagers.

In Germany during World War II, six million Jews died in the Holocaust. Nazi soldiers put Jews in concentration camps, tortured them, and gassed many to death.

It is no wonder, then, that Golda Meir left the United States with her young husband to live on a kibbutz in Israel. A kibbutz is like a commune. The people work together to make life pleasant. All have assigned jobs. Some work in the fields and farm, others in the nursery caring for young children. Still others cook or clean. All defend the kibbutz against attack by enemies.

Golda Meir soon saw that not only her kibbutz but all of Israel needed ammunition, food, and the goodwill of other countries. There was constant warring by those who thought the Jews had taken Israel away from the Palestinians.

Golda Meir wanted peace for her people. She worked tirelessly. Her husband seldom saw her, and they drifted apart. Her loyalty to Israel was so steadfast that she was willing to sacrifice personal happiness.

She appealed to the United States, her homeland, for help. When the U.S. agreed, she could hardly contain her joy. Israel had an ally, a friend!

Golda now began to make tours of the States to explain what Israel was up against. Her charm and sincerity, her obvious loyalty to her people came through, and she gained many followers, not only in Israel and the United States, but all over the world.

Golda, the young girl from America who had lived on a kibbutz, became Prime Minister of Israel. It was a glorious day,

Golda Meir is a prominent figure in the history of Israel because of her loyalty and dedication to that nation.

RTL

not only for her, but for the Jewish people. They were represented by a Prime Minister whose interest was not for herself, but for her fellowmen. Her loyalty rose to new heights, and she was valued for it.

- Golda Meir was diagnosed as having cancer when she became old, but she continued her job, ignoring her illness. What does that tell you about her?
- Did Golda want glory and power for herself?
- Describe the difference in the values held by Macbeth and by Golda Meir.

Isn't it wonderful to think about the brave and loyal men and women not only of the past, but of this century?

You probably want to reflect about the values that will make your life worthwhile. Not all our heroes or heroines were great leaders of countries or famous the world over. Some began just as you are beginning now to form your principles and values for a meaningful life.

Sheila Burnford

Canada, like many countries, has some very poor people. In Canada, many of the poor are Indians and Eskimos, whose lives are extremely deprived.

Sheila Burnford is a writer. She decided to write about the lives of Canada's Indians, showing their poverty but still also their character, their sense of survival, and their code of honor.

In a way, she followed her ancestor, John Phillip, who was a conservationist in the United States and worked for Indian rights, as well. Sheila Burnford used her talents to let people know that the Indians needed help.

She went to the reservations where the Cree and Ojibwa Indians live in the remotest part of Ontario. There she made

Children of the Ojibwa Indian tribe pose outside their new school in Ontario, Canada. The government hoped that the new school would reduce an 80% dropout rate.

CANADA
33

friends with Indian trappers and fishermen. She watched their way of life and listened to their stories. Then she wrote *Without Reserve,* explaining their needs. Many Canadians became more keenly aware of the help that was needed.

Sheila's loyalty to the first people to inhabit what is now Canada was steadfast. She had no fear of going to a lonely place in her country to talk with people to whom she was a stranger. She clearly gained their trust.

- Why is going to a remote part of Canada to understand the rights of the poor an act of loyalty?
- How did Sheila Burnford follow up on the stories told to her by trappers and fishermen?
- How did *Without Reserve* influence her readers?

The Boy Whose Name No One Found Out

In the late summer of 1989, in a small Midwestern town, a sudden fire erupted in the middle of the night in an apartment building.

It began slowly at first. Tenants continued to sleep until they heard screams coming from the second floor. A woman shouted, "The house is on fire!" By the time everyone woke up, the blaze had gotten out of hand. People were pushing and shoving each other in frantic efforts to escape.

A nineteen-year-old boy, who lived alone in a first-floor apartment, calmly dialed 911.

By the time the Fire Department arrived, it seemed that all had gotten out safely. The woman from the second story, who had alerted the others with her screams, had carried a three-year-old boy and a five-year-old girl out of the burning building.

She was sobbing, "My baby! I couldn't hold all three of them. My baby is upstairs!"

The small crowd standing outside tried to comfort her, but she was inconsolable.

"I just couldn't carry them all," she repeated.

The boy started to run toward the burning building. Firemen tried to stop him, but he eluded them and entered the building. The crowd hushed.

Within a few minutes he came out carrying a blanket-wrapped bundle. Quietly he handed the baby to its mother. Not only was the child alive, but the quick thinking of the boy — wrapping the baby in the blanket before running through the flames — had saved the child from burns.

The mother turned to the boy, tears of gratitude streaming down her face, but he was nowhere to be found.

- Why do you think the hero of this story didn't wait to be thanked?
- What was the hero's real reward?
- How is the value of loyalty involved in this story?

Jawahalal Nehru, Gandhi's Friend

Another great and loyal person of the twentieth century was Jawahalal Nehru.

You have read about Gandhi in Chapter 12. Nehru was Gandhi's friend and supporter when India was trying to become free of Great Britain. He too believed in peaceful negotiation instead of war.

During the struggle for freedom, the British drove tanks through the streets of India to frighten the people and to show military power. Gandhi ordered everyone to lie down in front of the tanks, and to set an example both Gandhi and Nehru did just that. Others followed and still others, until the streets were filled with people lying face down, daring the tanks to drive over them.

Of course, the soldiers did no such thing. It was a great victory for Gandhi and Nehru. The British were partially defeated, although the Indians never used a gun. Life was precious to Gandhi and to Nehru.

Many times, because of peaceful demonstrations, Gandhi and Nehru were arrested by the British. In jail, Nehru wrote about the struggle for freedom and his loyalty to its ideals. He never complained about being put in jail. He considered it a symbol in his peaceful fight for liberation.

Finally India became free, but turmoil developed. Some people were no longer true to Gandhi. They thought he had too much power. Part of India, known as Pakistan, broke away to form its own country. In spite of his great work, Gandhi was assassinated.

Nehru stood by his leader despite danger to himself and vowed to continue on the road to peace. His loyalty was not only to Gandhi, but to the newly freed citizens of India.

He became a hero to many, a man who could be counted on. Nehru carried on the work of the country, helping to create a democratic government. He became Prime Minister of India and was loyal to the teachings of Gandhi and the ideals of freedom.

- Why didn't Nehru mind going to jail?
- What does loyalty have to do with Nehru's being put in jail?

A Reflection on Loyalty

You can see that because you are a social being (you need family, friends, and a community), you are bound to form loyalties. Just the process of living together leads to feelings of belonging, which in turn lead to feelings of loyalty.

Some loyalties last throughout your life.

The culture you live in partially shapes your loyalty, but in spite of that, when you make a choice your values come basically from your conscience.

The Dilemma of Moses

You may know the story of Moses, the man who led his people, the Hebrews, out of slavery in Egypt three thousand years ago.

Moses was born the son of Hebrew slaves. Soon after, someone told the Pharaoh (dictator) of Egypt that a Hebrew baby might grow up to defeat Egypt and free the Hebrews. Pharaoh ordered that all newborn slaves be killed. Moses was just an infant, but his life was in danger.

To save Moses' life, his mother placed him in a basket and let the basket float down the river. She hoped that some kind person would discover the baby and save his life.

And that, so the story goes, is exactly what happened. The infant Moses was found by the Pharaoh's daughter, floating in his basket. The young woman was enchanted with the child. When one of the Hebrew maidens nearby asked if she intended to keep the baby, the Pharaoh's daughter agreed.

What she didn't know was that the Hebrew maiden was actually the sister of Moses. Without identifying herself, she asked the Pharaoh's daughter if she wanted a wet nurse, a woman who feeds a baby with her milk.

Of course, the answer was yes, or the baby would have starved.

Moses' sister ran to get the wet nurse, who was the real mother of the baby.

Moses was brought up in luxury in the Egyptian court. No one knew he was a Hebrew. He was treated as an Egyptian.

As Moses grew up, he learned the truth about himself — that he was not really an Egyptian, but a Hebrew. But since the Pharaoh's daughter had been good to him, he lived the life he was taught.

One day Moses walked far from the palace and discovered a camp of Hebrews. An Egyptian soldier was brutally beating one of them. Moses could deny his true heritage no longer. He defended the Hebrew!

Word spread swiftly about Moses. The Pharaoh, infuriated, asked for the death penalty for the boy he had treated as his son.

You know the rest! Moses led the Hebrews out of Egypt. His loyalty was to his people who had been treated as slaves.

We still thank Moses today for his tireless efforts in behalf of his people and for bringing the Ten Commandments from Mount Sinai.

He could have stayed in luxury under the Pharaoh's protection, but his true loyalty was to help free the Hebrews and to bring them laws and hope for a better life in the Promised Land.

He valued others above himself, and until his dying day he remained faithful.

- What is it that heroes and heroines who value loyalty have in common?

- How are truth and loyalty linked closely together in the stories of our heroes and heroines?

Mount Sinai

Thousands of years after Moses brought the Law down from Mount Sinai, a new question of honor and loyalty presents itself to people of the 1990s.

According to Exodus, a book of the Old Testament, the Lord gave the Law (Ten Commandments) to Moses on Mount Sinai. The Hebrews were supposed to have seen lightning, heard thunder, and witnessed the mountain smoking.

For over three thousand years Jews, Christians, and Muslims protected Mount Sinai. The Prophet Mohammed, Gamal Abdel Nasser, and Golda Meir saw to it that it was protected. They valued the mountain as a shrine.

About 30,000 visitors come to Mount Sinai each year and climb the steps built by Byzantine monks starting in the sixth century.

Now the Egyptian ministry of Housing and Reconstruction wants to build hotels and shops. To do this, they will have to bulldoze the wilderness of Mount Sinai, which means so much to various religious groups. There are 812 kinds of plants that grow nowhere except in those mountains. They, too, would be destroyed to make way for modern business. The businessmen clearly have no sense of loyalty to the millions of people who hold Mount Sinai sacred.

- What do you think could be done to help the Egyptians see that they are not doing an honorable thing by ruining Mount Sinai?
- Is business more important than the spiritual value many derive from a pilgrimage to Mount Sinai?
- If you could decide what to do, what would it be? How would your decision affect your inner self and others who need Mount Sinai as a spiritual place, unspoiled by modern technology?

Many people hold sacred the wilderness and religious buildings of Mount Sinai.

CHAPTER 15

Loyalty in Literature and Music

Have you ever read a book and wished it wouldn't end. You may have felt that the main character was very like you and been surprised to find somebody who thinks like you on important issues.

Books in which conflict plays a large part are hard to put down, not only because some of the characters are near your age, but because the tension of their struggle to adhere to certain values is so all-encompassing.

Many such stories deal with unusual people, but you are unique, too. You are unique because of your growing awareness of life around you and of your knowledge that the process of taking a position and sticking to it is difficult.

Huckleberry Finn

One such story is Mark Twain's *Huckleberry Finn*, about a young boy who struggled with values, too.

Huckleberry Finn's story takes place before the Civil War, when slavery existed in many parts of the United States. Huck lived in one of the slave states.

He did not have an ideal childhood. Far from it! He lived in a broken-down cabin in the woods outside a small town. He had no new clothes or even shoes. His father was an alcoholic; and, as you probably realize, alcoholic parents are often abusive.

In Huckleberry Finn's case, it was so. Huck was beaten so often by his father that when he was eleven or twelve years old he decided to run away.

It was a time of slave owners in the South, a time when preachers decided what was right and what was wrong, a time when following the rules of society was expected — without question.

Huck built a simple raft and began to float down the Mississippi River, hoping to get as far away from home as possible.

On the way he met many people. Often they talked about the moral issues of the time. They said that if a person steals property or commits other sins, that person is sure to burn in hell after death. Huckleberry Finn listened and continued his way down the river.

One night Huck heard a rustling in the bushes after he had stopped for the night. It was hard to see in the dark, but after a while he made out the shape of a man.

"What are you doing here?" Huck asked.

He found out! The man in the bushes was a runaway slave who was trying to make his way to freedom. In a way, wasn't that what Huck tried to do? To look for freedom from abuse? But in those days if you met a runaway slave the law said you had to turn him over to the authorities. Then the slave would be returned to his "rightful owner."

The slave's name was Jim. He begged Huck not to tell anyone that he had seen him. He also asked if Huck would share the raft with him.

Here it was — a question of loyalty! To whom should Huck be loyal? To a slave, who "belonged" to someone? Huck could hear the preachers and other folks in his head. They would probably say he was committing a sin, "stealing" Jim. He would surely burn in hell if he helped Jim.

On the other hand, Jim was a human being. He was more than a slave. He was a person in trouble and, above all, in search of freedom.

Huckleberry Finn had to make a choice — a choice in which his values were on the line.

As Huck tells his story: "I was trying to make my mouth say I would do the right thing and go and write to that nigger's owner and tell where he was; but deep down in me I knowed it was a lie, and He [God] knowed it. You can't pray a lie — I found that out!"

After a struggle with his conscience, Huck told Jim that he could share the raft.

"We said there warn't no home like a raft after all," Huck explains. "Other places do seem so cramped up and smothery, but a raft don't. You feel mighty free and easy and comfortable on a raft."

Together, Huckleberry and Jim continued their journey along the river, floating on the currents at night so no one could see them. They became close friends.

In the daytime Huck went ashore to find food. Sometimes he met people who made conversation about the runaway slave Jim. It seemed that many people were angry about the escape.

So Huck continued his struggle with himself, searching for the conclusion that would prove his loyalty.

Huck asked himself: Should I do what the "respectable" people say is right, and turn Jim in? If he did, he knew he would be betraying his friend.

Or, Huck asked himself: Should I be loyal to my friend Jim — loyal to what I feel in my heart was right? He knew that if he helped an escaped slave he would be "stealing." He would go to hell.

Finally Huck realized that he couldn't put off the decision any longer. "I was trembling because I'd got to decide forever betwixt two things," Huck said. "I knowed I'd studied for a minute, sort of holding my breath, and then says to myself, 'All right then, I'll go to hell.'"

- Huckleberry Finn's decision was indicative of Mark Twain's philosophy. Twain said, "Courage is resistance to fear, mastery of fear — not absence of fear."
- There is an inscription beneath Twain's bust in the Hall of Fame: "Loyalty to petrified opinion never yet broke a chain or freed a human soul."

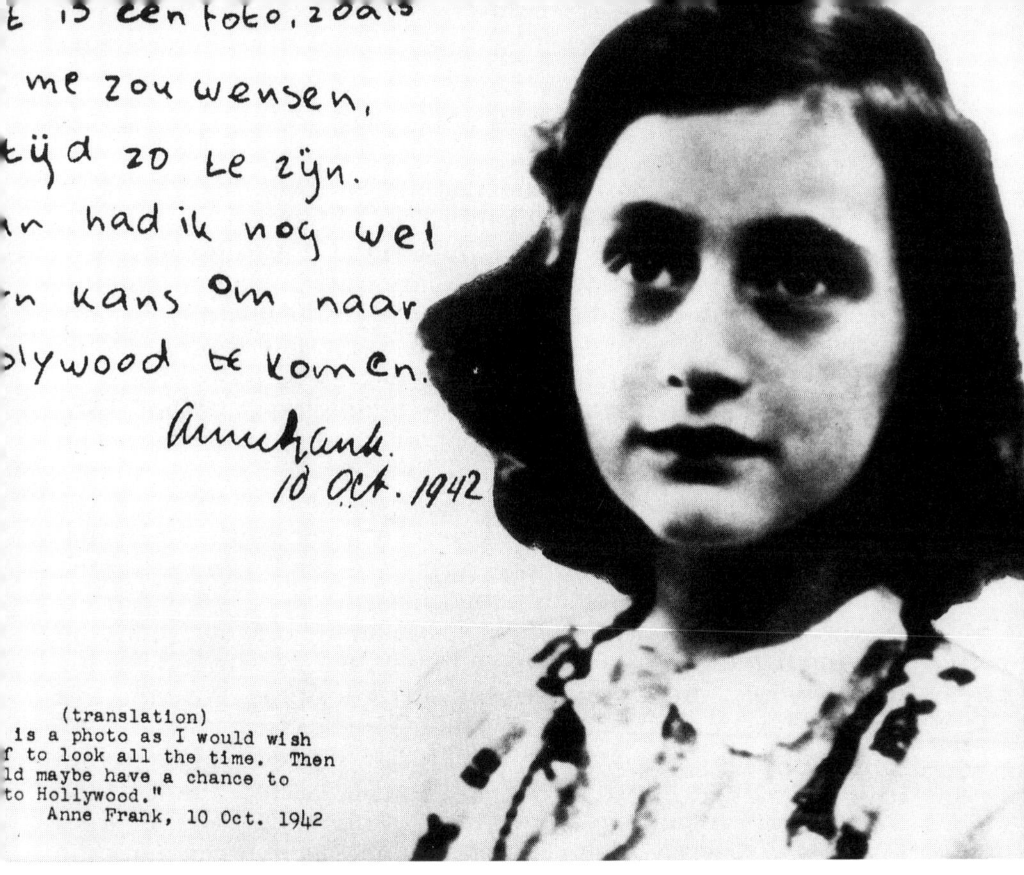

In her loneliness and isolation Anne Frank cherished this favorite photograph of herself and daydreamed of becoming a movie star before she was murdered by Nazis.

- How do you feel about Huckleberry's decision?
- What was he loyal to?

Loyalty in Time of War

In wartime people other than soldiers have performed almost miraculous acts of bravery and loyalty to their neighbors and friends.

One such time was during World War II. Perhaps you have read *The Diary of Anne Frank*.

It is the story of two Jewish families who hid from the Nazis during the occupation of Holland. They hid for several years in the attic of a combined office building and warehouse.

Anne, a young girl, wrote the diary to express her feelings, because life in the attic was extremely difficult for a young, active person. The two families had to be quiet every day, all day long, so they would not be discovered by the Nazis. They could speak only at night, when the building was vacant. They could not talk to anyone except each other and their kind Christian friends, Miep and Henk, who helped to hide them.

Sadly, after years of hiding, near the end of the war, the families were discovered and sent to a concentration camp. Anne, a teenager by then, was gassed to death, along with the others. Only her father remained alive.

The story of loyalty, however, is that of the brave friends who hid the two families. They knew that if they were found out the Nazis would not spare them the worst tortures. Why did this couple take such a chance?

They knew that Jews were to be "eliminated," to be gotten rid of by Hitler and his Nazi soldiers. They had heard of the concentration camps where men, women, and children were starved to death, worked to death, or gassed to death and then thrown into huge graves holding hundreds of bodies.

They did not want this to happen to the two families they sheltered. They could not conceive of such cruelty happening in their country, and they decided that their loyalty would be extended to these innocent Jews.

Not only did they provide a safe shelter for years, but they brought food, soap, gifts, and the necessities of life. Each time they entered the attic, they took their lives in their hands, but their loyalty continued unabated.

At the end of the war, Anne's father felt the need to return to the attic to have one last look around to remember his family and his friends.

As he stood in the now empty attic, Miep gave him Anne's notebooks. They had been found strewn on the floor. In them, Anne wrote of her feelings about growing up, her fear of being discovered, and of the great loyalty of the couple who helped them all.

A play was written about Anne Frank's diary by Frances Goodrich and Albert Hackett. They received a Pulitzer Prize for Best American Play.

When the play was performed in Amsterdam (where the story happened), Queen Juliana of the Netherlands attended the opening. People were sobbing, especially at the end of the play when the Germans were hammering at the door of the hideout. The audience sat in silence for many minutes. They could not applaud; they were emotionally exhausted.

- What is your reaction to the friends whose loyalty to Anne and the two families extended over the years?
- What is the interaction between faithfulness and bravery?

Cinderella

Learning values begins early in the lives of many children. You probably have heard many fairy tales from your parents, grandparents, and teachers.

Many of them dealt with the struggle between good and evil. You were most likely so caught up with the story that you didn't realize the power of the values that became part of you.

You remember the story of Cinderella, the girl whose wicked stepmother gave everything to her own daughters and nothing to her.

When Cinderella's fairy godmother allowed her to attend the ball, she and the prince fell in love. The glass slipper she left behind becomes a symbol!

It is a symbol of honor and truth. The prince, consumed with the idea of finding the girl who was honest and simple, undertook the search for Cinderella. He would have no other.

- Why would the slipper fit no one but Cinderella?
- The stepsisters were symbols, too — of what, do you suppose?
- Where does loyalty enter this story?

The Pearl

Have you ever wished very hard for something and when your wish was granted felt a kind of disappointment?

An example of such a wish involving the very soul of the hero is the novelette *The Pearl* by John Steinbeck.

The book is written almost as a fable. It is about Kino, a simple fishermen, his wife, Juana, and his baby, Coyotito.

The story begins on a quiet morning. Despite his poverty, Kino is content because he has the love of his wife and his infant.

Suddenly the peace of the day is broken when a scorpion stings Coyotito. It is possible the child may die.

Juana walks to town to seek the doctor's help. The doctor refuses because he considers poor fishermen like animals and he is not a veterinarian.

Kino and his wife and child go to their fishing boat. There, Juana places seaweed on the child's swelling shoulder while Kino dives for pearls.

Like a miracle, Kino finds his dream of dreams, a pearl so beautiful that he calls it the Pearl of the World.

As he shows the pearl to Juana, she is overjoyed but afraid that too much joy might ruin everything.

Suddenly Coyotito's swelling goes down. The pain leaves him, and Kino cries out at his good fortune.

Other fishermen and neighbors come to Kino's boat, and he shows them the pearl. He thinks he can now afford the best for his family.

From that moment on, evil follows Kino and his family. Jewelry dealers try to cheat him out of money for the pearl, his little brush house is burned by jealous enemies, and when he tries to leave town he is followed by murderers.

Coyotito is killed, and Kino realizes that the pearl has an insane music of its own and has brought evil and unhappiness to all he loves and values.

The very thing Kino wanted the most brought him the greatest unhappiness. He knew that he had to get rid of the pearl to remain loyal to himself and to Juana.

Kino threw the pearl back into the sea with all his might while Juana stood beside him holding the bundle of her dead baby.

They listened for the splash as the pearl entered the water.
Kino and Juana stood there watching for a long time.
The pearl disappeared.

Kino, again poor, his baby dead, found himself and his wife again, though he would never forget his beloved child.

- Why didn't Kino give the pearl to another fisherman?
- Whom could he trust with the pearl?
- To whom did he have to be loyal?
- *The Pearl* deals with the greater issues of good and evil. What are your comments? Could you find a friend or a group to discuss this question with?

Aida

For centuries people have been captivated by operas, which are plays set to music. The wonderful part of attending an opera is the music, which can tug at your emotions. You feel sadness, joy, or fear as the story develops.

One such opera, composed in the last century, is *Aida* by Giuseppi Verdi. Although Verdi was an Italian (the opera is most often sung in Italian), the setting of the story is Egypt.

It revolves around a handsome hero, Radames, who wins an important battle for his king. He brings riches from the land he conquered, horses, gold, and slaves.

One of the slaves is no ordinary girl. She was captured along with her father, who was king before Radames conquered his land.

Now Aida, the former princess, is a slave — and Radames falls in love with her.

Aida, too, finds a deep love for Radames, despite having lost her country.

At this point, the story becomes complicated. The music rings with the sounds of victory: The King of Egypt offers his daughter, Amneris, in marriage to Radames. It is an honor the king is bestowing upon his faithful soldier.

Radames is horrified! He loves Aida. Amneris sings of her delight. The king sings of the wonderful life that his daughter and Radames could have together. Aida sings a mournful aria

because she believes that Radames is lost to her forever.

However, Radames' love for Aida is true. Though threatened with death, he defies Amneris; he would rather die than live without his beloved.

Radames is sentenced to be sealed in a cave, there to die a slow, torturous death. As the cave is sealed, he makes out the form of someone else.

It is Aida! She is willing to share death with him. They embrace, knowing that their love will never die.

This kind of loyalty is often a theme of opera. Lovers die, and those left behind lead solitary lives forever — or die as well. The kind of loyalty shown in *Aida*, the idea of "until death do us part," is a rare and beautiful thing. How do you feel about the sacrifice made by Radames and Aida?

- What made Radames a true hero?
- Why do you think Aida was a true heroine?
- Why do you think he could give up the life of a prince for love?

La Traviata

Another opera by Verdi is one of the most popular because people identify with the sadness of the story and the beauty of the music. The music is so simple, yet so heartrending and easy to understand, that you could probably come away from a performance able to hum parts of it.

The story of *La Traviata* deals with the loyalty of Violetta. Violetta is a young woman of pleasure who entertains gentlemen. Her world is one of fun, laughter, and dancing, and Violetta is beautiful and popular.

One evening she meets a young man, Alfredo. He and Violetta are extremely attracted to each other, and they toast

Aida (seated), sings passionately of her love for Radames as the King of Egypt's daughter, Amneris, looks on.

each other with their wine glasses raised high, singing of the joy of life.

Actually, however, Violetta has a cough, which she tries to conceal from everyone. Alfredo finds out about her illness. He asks her to leave her life in the city and come to live with him in the country. She is in love with Alfredo and accepts. They live in the peaceful countryside and are as happy as two people can be. Violetta's health improves, and Alfredo is thrilled.

One day, Alfredo has business in the city. He promises to return by nightfall. Violetta knows she will miss him; it is the first time they have been separated.

No sooner has Alfredo left than Violetta's maid announces a visitor. It is Alfredo's father, Georgio Germont, a stern, disapproving man. At first Violetta is happy to meet the father of her lover. But when she discovers the purpose of his visit, she is crushed.

Germont first demands that she give up his son. Then he pleads that his daughter will never be able to marry well while her brother is living in such an irregular relationship.

Violetta protests that she loves Alfredo, that he is happy with her, but Germont is unyielding.

Violetta has to make a decision based on her love and loyalty to Alfredo. She decides that her loyalty to him can only be expressed by leaving him.

Quickly, she asks her maid to pack her things and leaves a hasty note that she is "bored" with country life and has returned to the city to her former life.

She is heartbroken as she leaves.

When Alfredo returns and finds the note, Violetta gone, the house empty, he becomes furious. He returns to the city to confront her.

Violetta is at a friend's house where a big party is going on. She is dressed in all her finery, and as Alfredo enters she pretends to laugh happily while her heart is breaking. Alfredo curses her in front of all the guests. His father is there, too, and tries to stop him, to no avail.

Soon thereafter, Violetta's illness gets worse. She has tuberculosis. As she lies dying, Germont realizes how noble Violetta really is and tells his son what he has done. Alfredo cannot believe his father's cruelty and rushes to Violetta to beg her forgiveness.

She is too ill, however, and has only a few hours to live. She dies in Alfredo's arms, as he sobs of his loss.

Violetta was loyal to the end.

- Despite her reputation as a flighty party-goer, Violetta was a woman who valued loyalty. If you had been in her position, how would you have handled the situation with Germont?
- How did Germont finally realize that Violetta placed the value of loyalty above her happiness?

PART FIVE

The Value of Loyalty: Making a Better World

Loyalty, as we have seen, is not a static value. True loyalty involves making choices. It requires a search for truth. It requires faithfulness to the truth that you find.

In the same way, when we practice loyalty we do not live in a static world. Our loyalty to each other and to our ideals helps us make our lives better.

CHAPTER 16

Loyalty as a Survival Mechanism

One of the most fascinating and gratifying aspects of human behavior is the way people help each other in times of need. Often a crisis brings out loyalty and the best in us.

Californians live under constant threat of earthquake. In October 1989, in San Francisco, one of the largest earthquakes on record struck in the middle of a peaceful afternoon. Suddenly, within seconds, bridges and houses collapsed. People found themselves homeless or hurt and helpless.

Those who were not hurt came forward, staying up all night to find survivors, to tend to the injured, and to serve food in hastily opened shelters.

In communities not struck by the earthquake, people banded together to make plans for emergency services when the "Big One," as Californians call the 8-points-plus earthquake still to come, will hit.

Neighbors have become "partners" with someone in their area to watch children, to collect water and food, or just to be there to encourage frightened people.

Community services, too, are getting ready to provide emergency services. Teachers are prepared to remain a minimum of thirty-six hours on the job to protect children as much as possible.

Volunteers search crushed cars for survivors after an earthquake in northern California.

In short, the threat of a natural disaster brings out positive values in people, values they often overlook in their busy daily lives.

It would be wonderful if we took some time every day to think of the helpless in our community. We do it in times of stress that involves us as well. Loyalty to one another need not wait for a disaster.

- What could you do to help someone during an earthquake or other disaster?
- What could you do to help someone in need if there is no disaster?

Loyalty to a Patient in the Family

In many homes you will find a patient with a chronic illness who is part of the family. The patient who is sick for a long time can try the patience of the family who are taking care of him or her.

The sad thing is that the patient is fully aware that he is a burden. What a way to go through life, realizing that the people he loves have to take care of him.

If you have such a person in your family, a sister or brother who is disabled or a parent with an illness that requires constant care, how can your attitude to them show love and loyalty? You don't have to do the job all by yourself, but you can give a word of encouragement, you can share stories of your day with the housebound, you can read a book to a lonely, bedridden person, you can make him feel a welcome member of the family.

Family Loyalty in Times of Stress

Have your parents ever come home from work tired, nervous, and stressed? They may express their exhaustion in a variety of unpleasant ways. They may seem angry or ignore you for a time while they deal with their stress.

If you become angry, too, the entire situation escalates and an unpleasant evening lies ahead.

This woman has just lost her husband. She will need the emotional support of her family to help her overcome her intense grief.

Your parents work to keep the household going. They are loyal to you. You can help by doing small chores without being asked, by having an occasional surprise for them.

But your loyalty will show itself most in your general manner of appreciation and love.

Of course, there are times when emotional stress reaches a far higher pitch than simply coming home from work exhausted. It could be the death of someone. Perhaps your mother's father died. She may be inconsolable, remembering her life as a child when he was Daddy to her. You remember him as Grandfather and will mourn him as well.

But your love for your mother and her suffering give you an opportunity to show how much you value her. You can comfort her and be with her a bit more than you ordinarily are.

There are times when the entire family is involved in deep emotional stress.

For example, a divorce splits a family apart. Some mothers and fathers ask their children to whom they will be loyal or whom do the children love more — mother or father?

That is an unfair question, and if you find yourself in such a position you need not answer it.

Your loyalty to your parents cannot be divided so easily.

What can you do? You can let them know of your sadness. Truth is always at the bottom of loyalty. And you can tell them you love them equally.

In moments of stress in your family, behavior that is low key and not hysterical is for the best. You can be supportive and do whatever you can that is comfortable for you.

- At times of emotional stress, to what must you first be true?
- How will your loyalty to your family show itself?

Loyalty to the Elderly

Before we discuss how we treat our older citizens in this country, you need to know that in Europe and Asia the old person is highly respected. He or she remains with the family

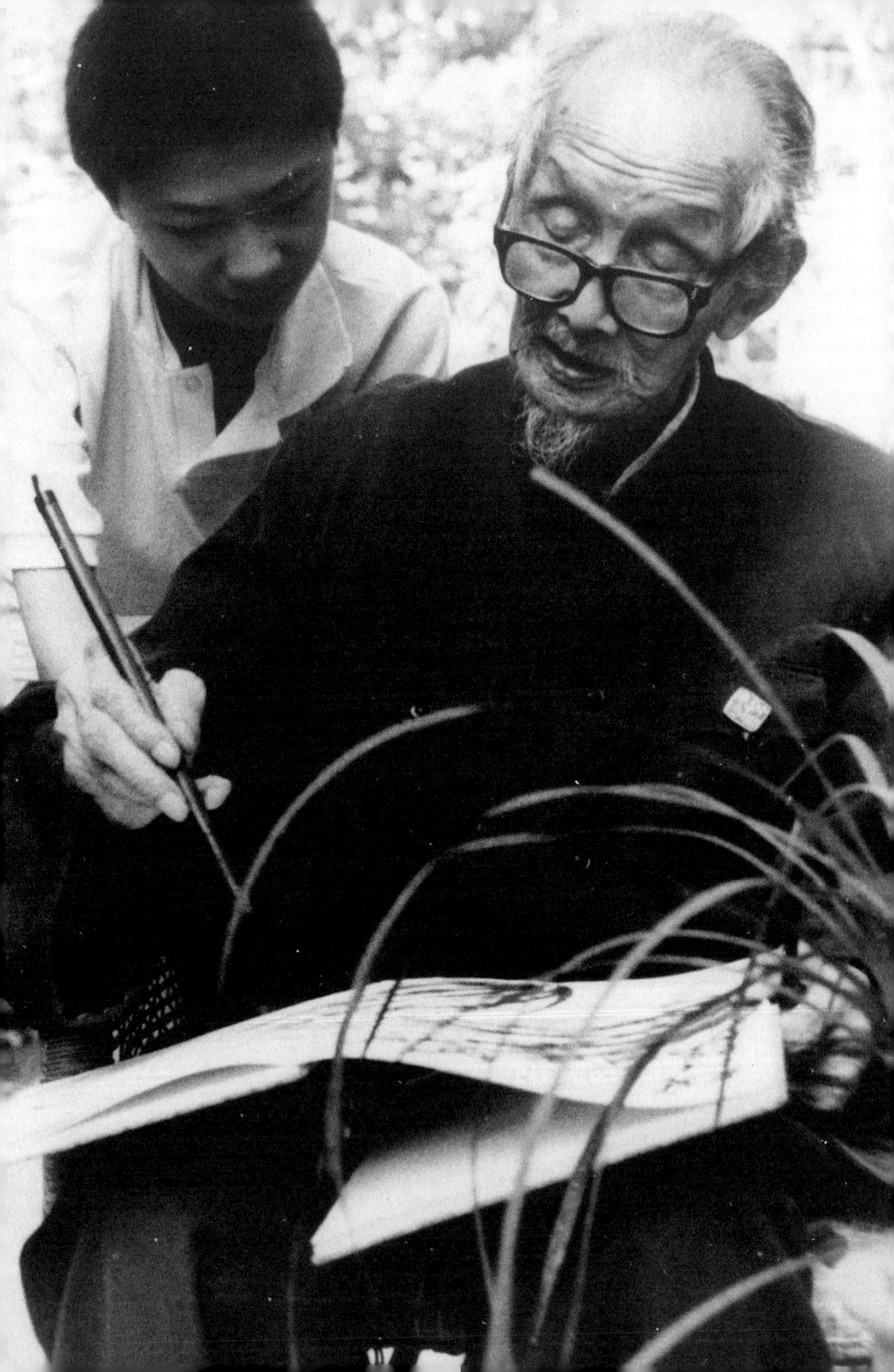

and is cared for by young and old alike. In many societies it is considered a privilege to care for an old person. Of course, there are nursing homes for the very sick and elderly, but families send them there only if the care is too difficult from a medical standpoint to continue to keep them at home.

Sadly, in our country, some have taken a strange position. Those who have elderly parents find a "rest home" for them when they can no longer live in their own homes, or when they show signs of forgetfulness and illness. The reasoning is that middle-aged people who have elderly parents are still working and cannot care for them.

Of course, in some instances that is a valid argument, but our nursing homes are filled with desperately lonely people who are neglected and receive few visitors.

You can help by raising the consciousness of your family. If you have a grandparent in a nursing home, put yourself in his or her place. Leaving someone alone is a sad thing.

Loyalty to the elderly is a noble cause. You and your family can make outings to the nursing home, perhaps even take the ailing grandparent for a ride, make him or her part of your life.

Some families, of course, keep the elderly in their home. It may be trying at times, because they need so much help, but remember that when you were small your grandparents gave you help.

The circle of loyalty is complete when we give back to the old person what has been generously given to us.

Above all, let them share in your life. They may be old, but they are interested. Don't shut them out. Be free and open with them, and the rewards of your loyalty will be heart-warming.

- Can you think of things an old person can teach you?
- How can you make an old person feel helpful and useful?
- Why is ignoring the elderly a negative value?

This Chinese man is one hundred years old. His expertise in painting and calligraphy are much admired by the younger generations.

SCOUTS OF AMERICA

Loyalty and Truth When You Witness an Accident

Many of you reading this book are already driving a car. No doubt you know all about defensive driving, politeness on the road, not driving after drinking, and other courtesies and laws of the road.

Suppose you have a best friend who recently received his license. He asks you to go for a drive with him. He is very excited, and you are happy for him. His parents generously lend the car for an afternoon drive, warning your friend not to drive in the evening on his first outing with a passenger.

The two of you decide to drive to a lake ten miles from home, but your friend laughs at the road signs.

"Fifty-five miles on this country road is ridiculous!" he shouts. "Let me show you the power of this car." He pushes the accelerator to 75 mph.

Suddenly a hitchhiker is standing in the road, thumbing a ride.

Your friend waves him angrily to the side of the road and loses control of the car. He sideswipes the hitchhiker, who falls to the ground.

"Stop!" you scream. "Let's see if he's hurt."

"Naw, he's just a dumb hitchhiker," your friend snarls. The power of the car has changed him. "Look, he's already getting up. I can see him in the rearview mirror."

As he stares into the mirror, he fails to watch the road and runs into a telephone pole. He doesn't seem seriously hurt but complains that his head aches.

What should you do?

You are about to make a decision regarding loyalty to your friend.

"Please," he begs, "don't tell my father. There's just a little dent in front. I'll have it fixed."

Should you lie for him when his father questions you?

This Boy Scout gets together with his elderly neighbor once a week to read to her. She is 107 years old.

Have you seen a side of your friend's personality you had not noticed before?

What is your responsibility to the hitchhiker, who has gotten up but looks somewhat dazed?

Could your friend have a concussion from bumping his head? What should you do?

Loyalty never stems from lies. You already know that. To be faithful to your friend, allow him to grow through this experience.

Report the accident. Call for the police and medical help. Your conscience, as well as your friend's, will be relieved.

One cannot dismiss a human being by saying, "Oh, he's just a hitchhiker." He is a person who was hurt by a car, and it is the driver's responsibility to make sure he is all right.

Your friend, too, needs to be checked. His instant headache may mean nothing much, or it could mean trouble ahead. As a good friend, should you take chances just so his father won't become angry?

As for the damage to the car, your friend's father has the right to know what happened to his property. Perhaps he will let his son pay for the minor damages, but that decision is in the hands of your friend's family.

- Will you be a better and more loyal friend by tellng what you saw as a witness to the accident?
- Whenever you are a witness to any car accident, should your evidence be for the person you feel the most sorry for?
- Would it be best to tell exactly what you witnessed? Why?
- In court, why do they swear you to tell the truth, the whole truth, and nothing but the truth?
- Truth is an aspect of ______.

CHAPTER 17

The Big Picture

The following questions are intended for discussion. You and a group of friends may want to grapple with these very serious thoughts.

1. What would happen if governments were loyal to all people?
2. What would happen if businesses were loyal to customers?
3. What would happen if families were always loyal to each other, not only in times of stress?
4. What would happen if you applied the value of loyalty to yourself?

These questions have to do with fairness, with giving up some things in order to receive greater value, a lasting value for life.

Why Is Loyalty of Such Great Value?

It is necessary to keep faith with those who have been faithful to you. That establishes trust and keeps relationships on a deep and stable level.

Thousands of environmentalists took part in the 1990 Earth Day March in New York. It marked the start of a worldwide movement against practices that threaten the globe.

Don't abandon old friends or allies for expedient new ones. If you abandon old friends for new, not only will the word about you spread, but your new friends, forewarned, will not form any kind of lasting relationship with you.

Similarly, if you have been faithful to others, it is necessary for them to continue to be faithful to you.

This two-way trust is one of the basic virtues of the value of loyalty.

Part of loyalty is putting the good of others above the good of self.

As we have seen from the actions of the wonderful men and women discussed in this book, they all put the good of others first, often at great risk to themselves.

Loyalty helps assure a safe environment, both physically and emotionally. Many scientists work hard to preserve our planet, to make nuclear power safe, to shut down factories that might affect the health of those who live nearby. Doctors are constantly searching for cures for heart disease, cancer, AIDS, and other life-threatening illnesses. They and many other environmentalists and quite a few politicians and ordinary citizens show their loyalty daily in assuring a safe environment.

Famous actors and musicians you may have heard of are doing their best to help our planet.

Barbra Streisand gave $250,000 to the Environmental Defense Fund for antinuclear activities.

Director Steven Spielberg plans to make a film about the destruction of the rain forests.

Sting, U2, Dire Straits, The Pretenders, Eurythmics, and Belinda Carlisle, as well as other rock stars, are contributing half the profits from their album "Rainbow Warriors II" to Greenpeace.

Paul McCartney is working with Friends of the Earth, another environmental group.

Meryl Streep helps Mothers and Others for pesticide limits.

Robert Downey, Jr., and Michael Landon have objected to offshore oil drilling.

Loyalty also gives you a secure sense emotionally. Your family, friends, teachers, ministers, and rabbis all try to provide you with love. They help you get a feeling of self-worth and teach you to be a good decision-maker. They surround you with constant care, and from it you learn the value of loyalty.

Loyalty is a value that stems from kindness. It replaces anger and hostility with positive forces such as faithfulness, dependability, and honesty. This value cannot be measured. It shows itself daily in your life.

Finally, loyalty is the road to peace. Two world leaders, Mikhail Gorbachev of the Soviet Union and George Bush of the United States, are beginning to dismantle many weapons to ensure a sense of trust among nations. The message is: If we, the "superpowers," do it, others may follow.

Elections are now permitted in countries where dictatorship had been the norm. Leaders find that they have to learn to trust

The two superpowers meet for talks to discuss ways in which they can cut back on nuclear weapons.

if they want to lead. They must place the good of people of the world above their own good.

The value of loyalty may save our planet.

Its road goes on and on, and you can walk on it. It is a safe road.

CHAPTER 18

The Emerging You—A Person of Loyalty

Will you be a loyal person? Before you can answer the question for yourself, you need to know who you are. You already realize that you are excited by the riches of loyalty, or you would not be reading this book.

Are you interested because a particular friend has caught your interest, because he can be trusted and you want to imitate him or her? That could be.

Maybe you admire someone in your family whose loyalty is steadfast, and you tell yourself you will become just like him. Your thoughts lead a path to yourself and what you think and feel.

Remember, as in all things, the value of loyalty has no "shoulds" or "musts."

"I should be loyal to my aunt because she is always so nice to me. She never forgets my birthday." If your thoughts lead you only toward "being nice to someone who has been nice to you," you are working on a false premise.

Loyalty stands alone as a value.

The kind of person you are or are becoming will automatically help you in the area of loyalty.

For instance, are you the kind of person who spends a lot of time doing what others expect you to do? They may be happy with you, but are you happy with yourself? Do you feel frustrated much of the time because you spend so much of it pleasing others?

Joan's Essay

Joan, a high school senior, decided to enter an essay contest offered at her school. The winning essay was to be read at graduation.

At dinner Joan mentioned her intention to enter the contest.

"Great!" her father's enthusiasm boomed across the table.

Joan was pleased because she had been sure that her father would like a competition that was intellectual.

Although Joan had decided to write on, "Growing Up in a World Without Communism," her father felt the topic was too political and not appropriate for graduation day.

"It's a day of celebration, after all," he argued.

"What would you like me to write about, then?" Joan asked, not letting her father know she was disappointed that he didn't like her idea.

"Oh, there are a number of things you can write about. I personally have great feelings for dolphins, and I'm afraid they'll become extinct if we continue to mistreat them. How would that be?"

"It's a wonderful thought, Dad," Joan answered, "but my topic is one I've taken notes on and read about."

"That's fine, dear, the more educated you are, the better. Do think it over. Promise Daddy?"

Before dinner was over Joan knew she would be writing about dolphins. And as it turned out, that is exactly what she did.

Her father's expectations had been met, but Joan felt painfully frustrated. Her essay was written listlessly and did not win the prize.

Most important, Joan had not been true to herself. Her

father's approval of her decision was no substitute for her own approval.

To grow into an independent and loyal person, you cannot be dependent upon others' needs. You have your own! They give you the strength to be faithful and to learn to become a person who values truth for its own sake.

Finding the Real You

To find your true self is to go on an exciting journey through your past. Throughout most of your life, you have been told and taught what to do. That is how most of us learn about our culture.

How you hear what you're learning sometimes makes the difference between making good choices or poor ones, between feeling dependent on the approval of others or trying new things independently, between choosing friends or being alone.

As long as you are a dependent person, you allow others to make decisions. Those others will choose your loyalties for you. Are they then yours?

You need to take a long, positive look at all your wonderful qualities. The first step is to be aware of yourself. Don't be too hard on yourself. Be honest as you evaluate yourself, but not too critical.

Once you realize that you deserve good things, that you are a worthwhile person, you begin to rely on yourself. You begin to be loyal to the person you are.

The same principle applies to making friends. Have you ever wanted to be a certain person's friend but given up without having made your wishes known?

"Oh, it won't last anyway," youn might have told yourself as an excuse.

You feel defensive and give yourself such reasons as, "I can't because," or "Bet no one else could get her to be her friend," or "Maybe you'd be like that, too, if..."

You are literally attacking yourself and not giving a chance to the person with whom you'd like to become friends. Are you being loyal to yourself, to your new friend?

Give others a chance by changing your behavior. Don't put yourself down. Instead, believe that what you want in a friendship is possible.

Is Anger a Sign of Disloyalty?

You may have heard your parents argue and thought, "If they were really true to each other and loved each other, they wouldn't fight." You see their disagreement as a sign of disloyalty.

Nothing could be further from the truth. Holding in anger is not honest. In fact, it makes you feel sick and anxious.

Psychologist Joyce Brothers says, "Anger repressed can poison a relationship as surely as the cruelest words." If you repress anger, there is bound to be an explosion.

If you want to be loyal to those around you and have relationships based on equality, a sharp word here or there won't hurt. It will establish your honest feelings because you take a risk when you express yourself. You are being loyal because you are allowing the other person to understand you. Your relationship can then move forward in a more positive fashion.

Should You Let Others Win?

Have you ever been in an athletic or scholastic competition? You entered it in the hope of winning. Suppose your best friend is in the same competition. Out of loyalty, should you step back and allow him or her to win?

Sandy and the Butterfly

Sandy, a twelve-year-old swimmer, had looked forward to the AAU (American Athletic Union) swim meet for months. She worked out four hours a day with her team and knew she was the best in her stroke, the butterfly.

In the dressing room her friend Chris said, "I'm going to

compete in the butterfly, too. Boy, are my parents going to be mad if I don't get first place!"

Sandy worried about it. Her parents would not punish her if she didn't make first place. Chris was her friend! Was her loyalty to Chris or to herself?

The day of the meet came. Chris was in Lane 3 and Sandy in Lane 4. Lane 4 usually had the projected winner. Sandy looked at Chris, who wiped a tear from her face.

At that moment the starting gun sounded. The girls dove into the pool. The race was on.

Sandy held back, but only for a few seconds. She felt uncomfortable in the slow strokes she took. She had to make her body move in the rhythm to which she was accustomed.

Can you guess what happened? Sandy won!

After the meet Chris had a talk with Sandy. "I was trying to make you feel sorry for me so I could win. Can you still be my friend?"

Sandy was astounded. She had done the only thing she knew how to do — be true to herself, swim fast — and now Chris let Sandy know she had done the right thing by winning.

She had been loyal to herself, not allowing her friend to manipulate her. Now the door was open to a close and true friendship between the two swimmers, a friendship based on real sharing.

Loyalty always contains the value of truth and honor. Falsely giving something up is not a virtue.

Guilt has no place in the value of loyalty. Had Sandy allowed Chris to win because she felt guilty, it would not have been a victory for either girl.

Gestures of Kindness

You realize by now that you don't have to be a great or famous person to practice loyalty.

Samuel Johnson wrote in one of his essays, "It is insufficiently considered how much of human life passes in little incidents."

That means that people don't pay enough attention to the many small but wonderful acts that happen daily.

It may seem strange, but if a person performs an act of kindness, it often has the effect of making others do the same.

Leland's Mother

When Leland was about ten years old his sister became very sick. One night Leland got up to get a drink of water. As he passed his sister's room, he saw that the door was slightly ajar and the light was on.

Leland tiptoed in. He saw his mother sitting in a rocking chair next to the bed, but she wasn't really doing anything. His sister was fast asleep.

Leland was scared.

"What's wrong?" he whispered fearfully. "Why aren't you in bed, Mother?"

His mother stood up and kissed him. "Nothing's wrong. I'm just watching over her."

This small incident had a profound effect on Leland. Years later, when he was an adult, a good friend became ill. The friend had no family, but Leland and his wife took him into their home and nursed him back to health.

Leland watched over his good friend.

Kindness, an aspect of loyalty, has a powerful effect that continues from person to person.

Love: A Cherished Part of Loyalty

There could be little loyalty without love, and loving is something you can do.

You don't have to be beautiful or talented or popular. Love is something you do to make lasting relationships and to make deep connections with people.

Dr. Viktor Frankl

Viktor Frankl was a Viennese Jew who lived during World War II. He was a psychiatrist. When the Germans came to Austria, he was separated from his wife and sent to a concentration camp for three years.

Every morning the Nazi soldiers inspected the prisoners. The sick ones were sent to the gas chamber to die. The healthy ones were sent to work.

Dr. Frankl shared two blankets with nine men and lived on ten and a half ounces of bread and one and three quarters pints of thin gruel a day.

One morning the workers — Frankl among them — had to walk for miles on the frozen ground to lay railroad ties. The guards hit them with their rifles if they did not move fast enough.

When a prisoner's feet hurt, he leaned on a neighbor's arm. The prisoners supported each other the best they could.

Frankl wrote:

> "As we stumbled on for miles, slipping on icy spots, supporting each other time and again, dragging one another up and onward, nothing was said; each of us was thinking of his wife.
>
> "Occasionally, I looked at the sky where the stars were fading and the pink light of the morning was beginning to spread behind a dark bank of clouds. But my mind clung to my wife's image . . .
>
> " . . . For the first time in my life, I saw truth as it is set into song by so many poets, proclaimed as the final wisdom by so many thinkers. The truth . . . that love is the ultimate and the highest goal to which man can aspire.
>
> "Then I grasped the meaning of the greatest secret that human poetry and human thought and belief have to impart: the salvation of man is through love and in love."

You are still a young person who is emerging into the loving and loyal being you will become.

You have been given a few tools to help you on your way, but your thoughts and actions, your feelings, and your growth toward honor will ultimately make you the person you want to be.

Bibliography

Anderson, Bernard W. *Understanding the Old Testament*, 3d ed. Englewood Cliffs, NJ: Prentice-Hall, 1975.

Curtis, Merle E. *The Roots of American Loyalty*. New York: Atheneum Publishers, 1968.

Frank, Anne. *The Diary of Anne Frank*. New York: Doubleday & Co., 1967.

Gunther, John. *Death Be Not Proud — A Memoir*. New York: Harper & Row Publishers, 1965.

McGinnis, Alan Loy. *The Friendship Factor*. Minneapolis: Augsburg Publishing House, 1979.

Royce, Josiah. *The Philosophy of Loyalty*. Reprint, R. West, 1985.

Schaar, John W. *Loyalty in America*. Greenwood Press, 1982.

Steinbeck, John. *The Pearl*. New York: Bantam Books, 1956.

Thomas, Norman. *Great Dissenters*. New York: W. W. Norton, 1962.

Twain, Mark. *The Adventures of Huckleberry Finn*. New York: W. W. Norton, 1961.

Wilcox, Desmond. *Americans*. New York: Delacorte Press, 1977.

Index